T0663741

A Year in Ink

Volume 8

San Diego Writers, Ink

A YEAR IN INK

Anthology Volume 8

Edited by reg e gaines and Dean Nelson

THE
INK SPOT
PRESS

A Year in Ink, Volume 8 is a publication of
The Ink Spot Press
San Diego Writers, Ink
NTC at Liberty Station
2730 Historic Decatur Road
Barracks 16, Suite 202
San Diego, CA 92106

Collection © 2015, San Diego Writers, Ink
Copyright for individual works belongs to the authors.

All rights reserved. No part of this book may be reproduced or transmitted in any form without written permission from the publisher.

Many thanks go to our many first readers and hardworking proofreaders. Special thanks to Kristen Fogle, Kim Keeline, Janene Roberts, and Matthew Phillips, Submissions Coordinator, for their efforts.

Cover image:
"Drive Home" by Margaret Larlham
www.MargaretLarlham.com

Cover and layout design:
Arin Winkler
www.WinklerDesigns.com

ISBN: 978-0-9799204-7-9
Printed in the United States of America
Printed by Lightning Source, Inc.

Contents

Prose Editor's Notes

Dean Nelson

This collection of prose from San Diego writers is a much better way of looking into what makes San Diego the way it is than any poll or survey could possibly accomplish. Reading these pieces was like looking into San Diego's medicine cabinet. Or its attic. Or garage. Or under the bed.

There is a collective imagination in this city that is breathtaking. Joy, pain, loss, achievement, love, betrayal—it's all here in an artful manner. The contributors have shown their ability to articulate the particular, which leads us all to our own experience. Their work assures us, frightens us, shows us another way to think about something, celebrates and bears witness. Most of all, though, their work *moves* us.

I am often asked if everyone has a story to tell. I paraphrase Flannery O'Connor, and tell them that if they have survived childhood, they have plenty to write about. They have a story. Not all stories are interesting, though, and not all stories are well told. Most people have stories to tell, but never tell them. It's easier to talk about writing than to actually write.

That's what sets this group apart from everyone else. These contributors did it. They didn't moan about all of the things that are keeping them from writing. They committed to the hard work of getting it on paper or screen. In my 20 years of directing the annual Writer's Symposium By The Sea at Point Loma Nazarene University, the most common statement all of these great writers utter, is that writing is hard work. They'd rather do something else. And yet they write.

And so do the people in this volume. They write well. They did the hard work. And when you read their work, I hope you have the same reaction I did when I read it, which is to exclaim, "Is this an incredible city or what?"

Dean Nelson
Director, Writer's Symposium By The Sea
Director, Journalism Program Point Loma Nazarene University, San Diego

Poetry Editor's Notes

reg e gaines

A title is crucial. Especially when given the responsibility of reading and selecting from more than 200 poems of such diverse rhythms and tones. It must allow the reader freedom to imagine, not serve as a sign leading to an exit ramp.

In making selections, titles were placed in A, B, and C piles, with poems subsequently read in that order. Next, a single pile of poems were chosen based on the writer's efficient use of language. This allowed very vivid imagery to sprout from the poem's page. Imagery and metaphor are crucial in today's world of brain dead rotation visual devices. It is as if these contraptions are now committed to destroying the beauty and importance of poetry.

The poem's experience as opposed to emotion was the final and perhaps most important requirement. Sights, sounds, smells, tastes, of unfamiliar experiences, allowed this reader entry into worlds I hardly know exist. The musicality, the architecture, the magnificent array of colors and strategic manner in which these simple stories are structured, made reading them all such a joy. Choosing one over another was purely an act of culture and craft colliding then collapsing on the page.

I am now responsible as a writer to have an even keener sense of awareness and thank all these dedicated poets and San Diego Writers, Ink for allowing me such an amazing artistic opportunity.

PEACE
reg e gaines

San Diego Writers, Ink

A YEAR IN INK

Anthology Volume 8

Saguaro

Christina Dorudian

Phantom hands reaching
Out of the ground
The Saguaro stretches
Fingers to the sky
Miles and miles
Of unanswered pleas
No one comes close
Too afraid to be
In their serrated embrace.

Suburban Dissection

Tina Barton

Upon examination
cul-de-sacs, schools
churches and tract housing
are lifeless objects
preserved in
suburban formaldehyde
appearing fresh
as a Madame Tussaud's creation
on its back
pinned down
skin sliced open
by a scrupulous scalpel
nonfunctional guts
are allowed to spill
a gray brain
washed sterile
an empty stomach
void of nourishment
embryos encased
still in a silence
and at its core
a dead heart exposed
memories of its pulse
worthless and forgotten
in this specimen of a town

Burying the Babies

Clayton Truscott

My girlfriend, an actual psychoanalyst, wants to know more about the public swimming pool incident. And I don't know what to say about it. Her brain is a machine that analyzes life in excruciating detail. Everything is meaningful. There are no accidents. If you let her run wild, she'll find a link between the way you order coffee and some hidden childhood trauma. This swimming pool story doesn't belong on the chopping block. It happened. That's enough.

I mentioned it about a month ago. Not the whole spiel, just the gory part that people are normally interested in. We'd only been seeing each other a short while and things were great. It was new love. Uncomplicated. Lots of red wine, late night talks, and playful sex. We were capping off a good day with a walk along Sunset Cliffs Boulevard, hand in hand, as couples do. We stopped south of Osprey Avenue to watch a group of teenagers playing on that cathedral-shaped arch of rocks above a deep channel. A natural high diving board. They waited for waves to rush in and collide against the rocks and then off they'd go, squealing delightfully. The ones who jumped first would bob in the choppy water, egging the others on to follow.

That looks fun, she said, would you do it?

I said no, just watching them made me feel anxious.

Why?

I mentioned the incident.

That makes sense, she said. Did you see a counselor about it?

No.

Again, why?

I got over it.

Really?

Before I could answer, the cops showed up to put a stop to the kids jumping off the rocks, and we moved on to another topic. The swimming pool story, in my mind, was cast back into its dark hole.

~~~~~~~~~~~~~~~~~~~~~~~~~~~~~~~~~~

I was five. It happened in Port Elizabeth, South Africa, where I grew up.

Grandpa Chuck was taking me on a special outing to MacArthur Baths, a public swimming pool center on the beachfront, just the two of us. I was upset because of something that happened at school.

We parked on Beach Road and made our way across the red pavement. Outside the front entrance to MacArthur's, we got King Cones from Rubber Face, the guy who sold ice-creams out of a cooler on his bicycle. We kids loved this particular ice-cream man. He was older, probably in his late fifties, and could make the funniest faces with his toothless mouth.

Hi scallywag, he said to me, what can I get for you?

I chuckled in anticipation of a show until we made eye contact; then I looked at the floor. It was the first time I can recall feeling ashamed of myself. I didn't want Rubber Face to know what I'd done.

He needs the biggest ice-cream you've got, Grandpa said.

Coming up, he said, producing a cone.

I reached for it with both hands, just as he inhaled a good portion of mouth and made his eyes bulge. Laughing made me feel better.

What do you say, Grandpa Chuck said.

Thank you, Sir.

You're welcome.

So off we went inside and Grandpa led me to the kiddies pool area. He took his shoes off and sat down with his feet in the water. I copied him.

He asked me about what happened. Tell the whole story, he said.

Woodrow Wilson hurt me, I said.

Woodrow Wilson?

Yes, Woodrow Wilson. I had no idea Woodrow was named after a former US president (I had no idea what a president was). To me he was just a bully with a V-shaped hairline.

How?

He stole my scooter.

That wasn't very nice. What did you do about it?

I struggled to answer this.

School policy said we couldn't ride a scooter for more than a few minutes, because there weren't enough to go around. Nobody was using them that day because it was too hot. I took the opportunity to try the red one—everybody's favorite. I'd never ridden it before and finally understood what the fuss was about. It was like flying. I kept going and going and going, and when my turn was over I went some more, because nobody was waiting for it. Until Woodrow Wilson saw me and realized I'd been on the red one for longer than usual.

He stood in my way and said, Hand it over, mine now.

I said he could use another one, there were plenty.

He said, No, I want *that* one. Rules are rules.

When I refused, he swung me around by my arm. I landed on the pavement, slapping my palms on the hard ground and grazing my shin.

Tears burned like wildfire across my cheeks as I watched him ride away.

~~~~~~~~~~~~~~~~~~~~~~~~~~~~~~~~~

At the end of recess, the teacher, Miss Wand, an ironically stick shaped lady, found me huddled in the dirt under the rabbit hutch. I was burying the babies. Woodrow was always trying to hold them too long (animals were naturally terrified of him) and my plan was to pin this crime on him. Which completely backfired.

Miss Wand couldn't handle the scene.

What have you done? she cried, pulling each one up from the sandy tomb I'd dug. All the other kids were sniveling and shouting at me, waiting to know if the babies would be okay. I scoured their worried faces looking for one: Woodrow's. But he was joy-riding on the red scooter, long after his turn should have been over, and missed the whole show.

I told Grandpa Chuck the story in as much detail as I could and said I was so, so sorry. I felt like a monster.

You know my boy, he said, putting his hairy arm around my neck, you might laugh about this some day. You're sorry and that's enough for now.

I shoved my face, full of ice-cream by then, into his chest and howled, hoping that was true because I knew it would be impossible to undo what had happened.

We sat there a while after finishing our ice-creams, watching people swimming and diving in the big pool, soaking up the afternoon glow. My parents were at home trying to get me into a new school, facing the awkward questions that parents endure when their son has been expelled for killing three school pets. Miss Wand made sure that I was gone.

The hot tiles began to shake under some heavy footsteps and the sound of running caught my attention. I looked up and saw Rubber Face thundering toward me, wearing only his raggedy underpants, which hung low on his scrawny, malnourished frame. He launched himself into the kiddie pool and for a micro-moment we locked eyes again. He was pulling a famously funny face, which detonated a burst of laughter in my belly, before he landed headfirst in knee-deep water. And then I watched his body sway into stillness as the final ripples lapped the side of the pool and everything slowly turned red.

~~~~~~~~~~~~~~~~~~~~~~~~~~~~~~~~~

We meet at her house after work. It's evening now, close to sunset. She lives on the other side of Ocean Beach, the noisy side, and wants to take her new dog for a walk. A big, burly, rust-colored mutt, Rojo. I was there when she chose him over a hundred other cuter, younger, more appropriately sized dogs with cheaper medical needs. I found her decision noble but hoped that our relationship wasn't based on the same selection process.

He's no show dog, but there's something beautiful about his simplicity. When Rojo's in a good mood he wags his tail and grunts and dances around slowly, otherwise he just lies there waiting to be fed or walked. It's easy to like him and to be liked *by* him, but I don't want to get too attached. Partly because she might can me at any time and partly because he's only got one or two good years left before his bad hips fall apart. I feel like we're allies on the same mission, though. We're both in love and just want attention from her; we wait patiently together in the kitchen while she gets ready.

The psychoanalyst, Rojo, and I finally set off for Dog Beach. She lets him off the leash when we get there and leans her head on my shoulder. Rojo turns to us, almost asking for permission to run, and then waddles toward the water.

Tell me again about the public swimming pool incident, she says, breaking away to follow her dog.

I tense up and express my desire not to speak about it to her.

I don't want to analyze this—it's just an interesting story about you. I care about *you,* she says.

You can't help overthinking it, I say.

Yes, I can.

I'd rather not.

An awkward silence falls over us. She gets this focused look on her face, like she's now analyzing my response, weighing and measuring this omission on the scale inside her head, assessing its significance in the Big Picture. A worthy man talks about his trauma, I imagine her thinking—which doesn't sound like her at all.

So I end up telling her the story, pretty much the same as the way I told it above.

Just as I'm getting near the end, she stops me and points.

Rojo is circling a spot in the sand, close to the river mouth. He's really excited; barking and peeing *everywhere*. Once he's saturated his spot in an acceptably foul layer of urine, he starts digging at full speed, working like there's a second chance at youth buried in the sand. Digging with more energy than he has to spare.

I try talking again, but she stops me and says, Wait, look at Rojo.

I instantly feel wounded that she's not respecting the dollop of trust I'm serving up, but Rojo's behavior is puzzling enough to keep me distracted. Other dogs gather at the spot too, digging manically like him. They're all excited to get to the bottom of some hidden mystery.

More people and dogs show up; there's a crowd now. Everyone is watching and waiting. People get their cameras ready.

And then this Alsatian finds whatever *it* is and excavates the treasure. In the dog's mouth is a decaying skunk that is missing half its face and is covered in maggots. The smell is immense. Everyone standing there does a 180 in unison, like we've all been slapped in the face at the same time. But the dogs go completely bananas, barking and wailing and digging for more; as far as they're concerned, the most valuable thing in the world has just been uncovered on Dog Beach.

Poor old Rojo is furious. He growls and flashes his teeth at the Alsatian, and wrestles the skunk away, wielding a dominance he might have known as a younger dog. Rojo seals the deal by rolling on the skunk's corpse, making sure he is wearing the chief's perfume now.

The psychoanalyst intervenes by smacking Rojo's snout. No! Bad, Bad Dog! she shouts.

The poor old boy is utterly bewildered. He doesn't understand why we're leaving in such a hurry or what he did to piss her off.

We're walking back home with a freshly laid wall of silence between the three of us, Rojo and I on one side, our psychoanalyst on the other. I don't know if she's pissed about

Rojo snapping or the fact that we're going to have to wash the smell off him.

I try to grab her hand, but she bats it away angrily and this stresses me out.

I can't take another moment.

What? What did you think of the goddamned pool story? You can't force me to talk about something like this and then say nothing!

She looks at me, puzzled, irritated even and says, You were a lucky kid. Is Grandpa Chuck still alive?

Like Rojo, he is.

As we march on toward her house, the sunset glows all around us, bathing everything in light red, while storms brew somewhere in the distance.

Cut to the Quick

Lynn Gahman

I was perched on a loveseat in the atrium bar, wearing a little black spaghetti-strap chemise, wafting "Forbidden," my signature scent. A three-piece penguin band played softly in the background as I sipped chardonnay.

I nervously twirled a curl around my finger. I hadn't meant to flaunt my indiscretion. Like so many others, I thought I'd get away with it.

Or even more cliché, maybe I'd wanted to get caught. After all, the grand opening of the Radisson was bigger news than the town's new Walmart.

The band had just swung into "The Second Time Around" when Michael walked by. His face registered the stages of betrayal: Surprise. Hurt. Anger? A feeble attempt at recovery. That was the saddest part.

My face flushed. *Idiot!* I hadn't given a thought to how Michael might feel. I'd been focused on myself, *my* wants, *my* needs. How could I have been so selfish?

Yes, lately I'd been bored. Looking for something new. Something different. Something exciting.

I flashed back fondly to our easy conversations. At one time, I could tell him anything. But this time, I'd never found the right words. I should have told him what I needed.

I walked over and blew an air kiss beside his cheek. He looked numb. He introduced Maureen, his wife. A smile seemed etched into her face. She *knew*.

Of course, I'd heard all about her. He'd talked a lot about his family. Mercifully, they moved on. Guilt and remorse flooded me.

I settled back on the loveseat and pulled out my iPhone, searching the Internet for rationalization. Turns out 65 percent of clients cheat on their hairdressers. Most of us come to regret it, unable to live with the guilt. Or just unable to live with our hair. Two haircuts later, I still struggle with a spot in the back.

More guilt. More remorse. The answers could not be found in a single glass of Kendall-Jackson. I needed help. I swiped the onscreen keyboard.

Dear Dr. Phil...

Three Stitches

Ron Salisbury

Not the gruff voice leaping out of a doorway
at 2 AM with a Buck knife, not the sharp rim

on the bonnet underside of an antique Jag.
Not the spike from the broken plate when

the second wife left, no kick from a rooster,
slip of a pearl handled boning knife at thanksgiving,

a straight razor, shaving before the awards,
or the thin edge of her zipper, after.

But trimming the root end of a celery stalk
before lunch for one, the lonely sun smudging

the table, oil for the salad, arugula, pico de gallo,
avocado, tomato. Henry Purcell's Dido and Aeneas

filling the room like a dirge and I'm thinking of us
in Venice or was it the Pegasus Vineyard in Napa,

the knife slicing through memory like a quick dog
catching a scrap. A reminder to pay strict attention

to what I have now and leave the rest for a time
free from self-pity and away from sharp things.

Vietnam Dawn 1968

James M. McCollum

sun cracks flat horizon
fire fills sky
warm air warms
black clad figures
trot feet beaten trails
morning silence broken
by distant snap
of sniper's round
woman squats
in long shadows
of early morning
inside rusty
whirling wire fence
(shit) life burns in
cut diesel drums

Crash

Elizabeth Forsyth

¿Sabes cómo jugar al fútbol?"

"What?"

"¿Sabes lo que estoy diciendo?"

"No habla Español." He knew that phrase.

His cousins laughed at him. His second cousins. One kicked a soccer ball toward him, which he kicked back with his toe. The ball lifted and fell, stuttering on the ground, rolling halfway back to the cousin it came from. The cousin kicked it back to Ed, with an exaggerated turn of his leg and a kick of the ball with his instep.

Soon Ed was assigned goalie, which caused some of his cousins to fight with other cousins.

His mother stood on the sidelines, observing the game. The rest of the mothers, uninterested in the game, spoke with rapid Spanish inside the house, their laughter joining with the yells of the kids.

Ed tried to keep up with the game, looking at the ball, watching it pass from cousin to cousin. But somehow he lost track of the ball, watching the tangle of his cousin's legs, and spotted it coming toward him too late.

The ball crashed and scraped into his face, leaving marks on his chin and indenting his nose. The tears rose, unbidden, and his chin hurt as it wobbled.

Ed's mother came rushing to his side, moving past his cousins who gathered to stare. The cousins pushed and shoved to get a better look at the blood that was beginning to drip from his nose onto his lips, which would look pretty awesome and gruesome to the nine-year-old cousins obsessed with gore.

The tears continued and the fascination of his cousins grew to embarrassment for Ed. Their mothers didn't wipe their tears and pull out portable first aid kits from a fanny pack. Their mothers hadn't been watching from the beginning, looking for any hint of danger. Their mothers would hear the cries and deem them unimportant enough to come out. They knew the difference in their child's cries between a bruised nose and a broken one.

"Are you ok? You guys were playing a little rough."

The cousins didn't understand what Ed's mom was saying, but they could feel the reprimand as she looked in their direction, a slight frown on her face. They shuffled, hiding behind each other, still filled with giggles after the rush of adrenaline from playing and a player being injured.

She poured some alcohol from a mini bottle onto compressed cotton pads. She dabbed Ed's nose and chin with one, and he pulled back, stinging from where his skin had come into contact with the alcohol, the tears flowing freer.

"This should be washed, but the water here…"

She shook her head, as if stopping herself from saying anything bad.

"Let's just go rest, Ed."

His sister was still a baby back then, and his mother had loved naptimes. They lay in the bed, the fan pushing cool air over them, a costly American extravagance, for the American guests of honor.

Looking back, it was clear that his mother just wanted an excuse to get away from it all, especially the noise, and they fell asleep together on his parent's bed, dreaming of a return to a world where they weren't special.

Cuernavaca

Carrie Danielson

My sharpest memory of that day in Cuernavaca was the gold sparks and blue flash that I thought at first were little hand-thrown fireworks, but instantly sensed were something more dangerous and different. I saw the two boys, Miguel and David, in a staccato dance, an arm jerk here, a leg, a grimace. And then they fell, like wrestlers in a desperate embrace in the dark, in the shallow pool of water that filled the intersection of the two little streets in the pueblo. Too late we realized that there should have been light; there should have been street lights to illuminate this bizarre scene, now becoming macabre in the most terrifying way. Too late we knew what we desperately did not want to know. And when the flames erupted we stood in silence, aware that they were gone and that if we had taken one more step, just one more, it would have been us too—burning and dying as the power line flickered, buzzed and flashed like a sparkler in the night—a neon sign, illuminating the frozen horror on our young faces, now aged with grief.

A Chance to Dance

Tim Calaway

a dance
a chance
to hold
you
once again
familiar feel
our hands
together
fingers entwined
music
of an old movie
slow and plaintive
rides with me home
from your wedding

1969

Debbie Hall

you weren't what mama
had in mind—maybe a lighter
shade of militant could
have been—but I marched
to the dark side, reading Malcolm
and Eldridge in the crook
of your love
and with a honed glare
told those cops
nothing is wrong with my car and
this-brother-is-my-friend-
can-we-go-now

and I was in love
with your righteousness
and my borrowed indignation
my whiteness cloaked
in layers of cool
practiced and worn
with your pride

and we danced
in a roomful of sway
humming souls touching
sweet-salty limbs
in a snake-coiled groove

and I loved Aretha and Marvin
and Otis too

so how did this end
with your fist in my windshield
gun in your pocket
tears in back
of your rage?

All That Isn't Singing

Judy Reeves

CHAPTER ONE

S mith's Fishing Camp, Lake of the Ozarks, smack in the middle of the State of Missouri was not where Louise Guest planned to be that summer of 1957. But there she was, just after sunset under broad trees strung with festive colored lights at Smith's Annual End of the Season Fish Fry. From the bandstand, honky tonk music sent out its lusty invitation to dance, to feel good, to let it all out in one final whoop of summer freedom.

Louise plunged her hand into the ice-filled washtub to grab a Coke, popped the cap with the opener chained to a handle and slipped into the shadows behind a tree. She spilled a dollop of Coke on the ground and refilled the bottle with a serious shot of bourbon from a beat-up flask and leaned against the tree, its bark rough against her skin. Peering through the tangle of couples shuffling on the dusty patch of make-do dance floor, she watched her mother dancing with that cowboy, someone Louise had never seen before, and neither had anyone else. Her mother, all dolled up in a green dress that fell in soft folds against her legs, smiling up at him and his hand spread wide on the small of her back where Daddy's hand used to be, should be, would be if he wasn't in California instead of with them.

The flask slid easy back in its little cloth sack. She pulled the drawstrings closed and balanced it in the tree where she'd stashed it earlier. With a little tug she adjusted the knot of her shirt, her favorite white cotton with cowboys embroidered on the pockets and tied just at her belly button. Blue Capri pants, ballerina flats, hair fair as moonlight—that's what her daddy said, "fair as moonlight in January"—brushed up into a French twist.

Men liked to look at her, she knew that. All summer she'd been practicing her moves. *Sultry* with poor Hiram in the filling station, the smell of his bait tanks as bad as the stink of oil from his garage. Hiram wouldn't know sultry if it had a steering wheel and horn. *Flirty* with Butch the Wonder Bread man who delivered hot dog and hamburger buns to the café every Monday and Thursday. Butch wasn't as old as her daddy, but he'd been in the War, too. He still made jokes about the Japs, called the Germans "krauts."

Up on the stage making all that music was Ruby Diamond in her red fringed shirt and her hair lit up like a bonfire. "Ruby Diamond and the Gemstones." Ruby, with her whiskey voice and faraway eyes that made Louise think about things like stealing that Pontiac from Hiram's Garage and hitting the road. Ruby Diamond, with her high cheekbones that she said came from her Cherokee grandmother and fine nose that was probably from her family's Spanish side, "Conquistadors, doncha know," and that blaze of red hair from her Irish ancestors. Ruby Diamond, with all that foreign blood running through her veins, the best thing America ever made as far as Louise was concerned.

They'd been at Smith's Fishing Camp three months, ever since her mother loaded her and her sisters in the car with nothing but their clothes, and headed south instead of west, everything else they owned on its way to California where her daddy had already started his new job writing about sports for the Los Angeles Times.

She sipped her Coke, getting use to the burn of the bourbon, the cheap stuff siphoned from Hiram's supply kept along with the sweetbait and minnows for early morning fishermen.

"Louise. Hey Louise."

She looked up into the deep shadows of the tree. Roseann, her little sister, sprawled out along one of the branches, half hidden in the dark. Twelve years old, hair dark as a crow's wing (that's what Daddy said), Roseann knew the name of every tree, wild flower and weed in the state of Missouri. She fashioned bracelets from sweet clover that she gave to Louise and the women at the camp, and kept baby mice in matchboxes with nests made from leaves. Louise's mother called Roseann her "wild child."

"What are you doing up there, kiddo?"

"Just watching," Roseann said.

Roseann wasn't as much of a watcher as Anna, the third and youngest Guest girl. Six years old and never without her Big Chief tablet and pencil, making notes. She wanted to be a writer like Daddy. You didn't want Anna around when you were practicing your moves.

From her vantage point in the tree, Roseann had a better view of the dance floor than Louise, but still Louise could see her mother and the cowboy dancing. The smile her mother was giving him was one Louise hadn't seen all summer long.

They'd been arguing off and on all day, Louise and her mother. With fall coming the fishing camp would be closed for the season, the café along with it, and her mother was seriously considering a job driving a school bus.

"A *school* bus," Louise had said earlier that afternoon, the two of them on the screened porch of their cabin with its cobwebbed corners and beat up furniture. "You barely know how to drive a car. Why can't we go to California now?"

"Because I say so."

"Because of what happened between you and Daddy." Same argument, different verse.

"That's none of your business, Louise." Her mother stood solid, hands on her hips.

"It *is* my business because I'm supposed to be in California." Louise's own hands on her curvy, I'll-be-18-in-November hips. Her green eyes into her mother's brown ones and neither giving up a blink.

"You're supposed to be where I tell you to be," her mother said.

It wasn't just the summer they'd been at each other. Louise couldn't remember a time when they hadn't argued. "You're my challenge," her mother had said to Louise. "You're my cross to bear." One especially hot spat she'd said, "I hope you have a daughter just like you so you'll know what its like."

"I'm not having any daughters," Louise told her.

Even then Louise knew she was going to be a singer, the kind of singer who wouldn't have time to be a mother. She dreamed herself singing in clubs, fantasized singing on stages with bands. She'd sing in movies and on records. If there was any place in the world where a singer would be, that's where she would be.

So no matter what her mother said, Louise was not about to ride a school bus fifteen miles to some hick school in some throwback country town. In her best fantasies, when they wrote about her in *Photoplay* or *Silver Screen* they would say, "Louise Guest graduated in 1958 from Hollywood High."

"Tell me if you see anything interesting, Roseann," Louise said, though Roseann probably didn't find who their mother danced with at an outdoor party of much interest. Louise edged around the dusty patch of dance floor. Hiram and some of the fishermen hung together in a beefy knot by the grill with Butch the breadman and Carl, the gangly kid who fell out of a tree earlier that summer and broke his arm.

Butch had asked her to dance a couple of times that night. He danced like her daddy, with an extra step to the beat and every now and again sending her out in a spin and a twirl under his arm. With Daddy you knew when to expect that turn; he had a rhythm, a routine you could count on. With Butch, you never knew when to expect it, he just flung you out any old time.

She skirted wide around the men and cut across the corner of what used to be the back lawn that angled down to the lake.

The honky tonk sounds of the Gemstones, and Ruby up on the bandstand in her fringed shirt and silver boot tips flashing in the lights, just made you want to dance. Sometimes Ruby'd take the microphone out of its stand, and dance a side step slide right along with you.

Louise had never sung with a band, only with the piano at school talent shows, and with the radio, and records on the hi-fi, shaping the words like the singers did, mimicking their phrasing. She'd been practicing to be a singer forever. And, since she'd met Ruby Diamond, she wanted to be a singer just like her.

Ruby Diamond waited tables at the café on Tuesdays, Louise's mother's day off. That's how they knew each other. Louise washed dishes every day—another thing she could thank her mother for, a summer of washing dishes in the café, but at least she could save a little money; nothing to spend it on at the fishing camp.

One of those Tuesdays earlier in the summer, that time between lunch and dinner when the café was empty, Ruby and Louise were doing those in-between chores—filling sugar containers and napkin holders, dripping catsup into red squirt bottles. The radio above the stove in the kitchen turned up loud enough they could hear it in the dining room. Louise wasn't even aware she was singing along when Rosie Clooney came on. *Jambalaya and a crawfish pie mi-o-my-o.* Ruby, her hand still stuffed inside a napkin holder, said, "Well, listen to you, Miss Hit Parade. Where you been hiding that voice?"

That started it. Tuesdays became the only day she looked forward to—Ruby Diamond in her wedgies and silver bracelets, her red hair in a scarf like it was held back against its will, waiting tables and telling Louise stories about singing with a band, being on the road, record contracts and road houses. Nashville, Tennessee; Austin, Texas; and *Yeah, I been to California. All them palm trees and sunshine. Too much light for me.*

Louise leaned against a picnic table next to the bandstand, listening to Ruby Diamond up on the stage, the band behind her—Stu on drums, Buddy on steel guitar, Lester on the slide. Man-oh-man, she ached to be on that rickety stage under those colored lights. Ruby Diamond's red hair flashing and the fringe on her shirt swinging, singing /*I go out walking*/ side step slide/ *after midnight*/ step step, the silver tips of her boots glittering like they held stars inside.

Louise couldn't help but sway her shoulders in time to the music, anybody with an alive bone in their body would do the same, and the next thing she knew she was singing the words right along with Ruby. Lester looked up over his slide, and gave her a grin, and Ruby—side step side step—right over to Louise. She didn't stop singing a minute just crooked her finger with its bright-as-a-stoplight polish right at Louise, like "Come on up here, girl," and Louise, eyes wide, pointed her own brightly painted finger at her chest and said, "Me?"

Ruby wiggled her finger again. *Come on up, come on up, come on up, Louise,* she sang.

Louise climbed the riser to the stage. It was only a foot or so high, just one big step, but she felt like she was being lifted by some magic force. Ruby put her arm around Louise's waist, pulled her close so they could share the microphone. She smelled like sweat and whiskey, and Louise swore she'd never smelled anything so sweet in her life. Ruby led into the verse / *I walk for miles*/ hip bumping into Louise's / *out on the highway*/ and Louise joined in, her face so close she felt the brush of Ruby's hair against her cheek. Man-oh-man, did it feel good to sing like that, better than the talent contest at school, tons better than standing in front of the mirror watching yourself. Singing and Ruby's sweet whiskey voice right in her ear. Maybe Louise didn't believe in God, she still wasn't sure, but she did believe in that angel voice. And wouldn't Ruby give a big hee-haw to hear Louise describe anything about her as angel-like.

Louise was all feeling—the swell of her voice in her throat, her heart going like mad, Ruby's voice sweet in her ear, the mellow notes of the guitar. Images of people in the audience appeared as if captured in the flash of a camera: Velda fanning herself with a paper plate at a picnic bench with Agnes from the phone company. Over by the barbeque, Hiram and Butch and the other men. There was Roseann stretched out on her branch like a sleek cat. Millie and Helen, the spinster twins from down the road dancing together. In front of the stage, Anna dancing by herself, wearing a big grin like she couldn't keep it in.

And out under the leaning branch of a far tree another picture: Her mother turned so her back was to the stage, all her attention on that cowboy, like it wasn't Louise up on the bandstand singing with a real band for the first time in her life.

She stumbled over the words. Ruby squeezed her waist, sang the line louder. Louise picked it up again and she was back in the song, back where it felt like she belonged. Sweat shone on her now, too, and the sound surrounded her like the light from those colored bulbs shining down. She was a kaleidoscope of light and sound and music and song.

Then it was over.

The applause roused up and Ruby leaned into the microphone and said, "Now don't that little girl have a voice?" More applause and Anna yelled out, "Yay, Weezie," and it was that feeling like you want to explode, feeling so good.

"Thank you," she said, suddenly shy and grinning. Ruby gave her a wink and that sealed it, like Ruby'd just taken a picture of what Louise's whole life was laid out to be.

The band pick up again, Stu's brushes soft against his drum as if the world hadn't really stopped. Ruby took the mic out of its stand and held it close to her mouth, *Crazy*, she sang, *Crazy for feeling so lonely.*

Louise stepped off the stage, feeling a little dizzy, and Anna bounded up and grabbed her hand. "You were good, Weezie." Velda and the women at the picnic table with their fans and flowered dresses, all smiles and nods.

A few yards away, apart from the other couples, her mother and the cowboy were close-dancing. The man's back was to Louise, her mother's hand touched his neck. Even from where Louise stood, even in the falling dark, she could see her mother's eyes were closed.

The glow of being up on the stage, cheek-to-cheek with Ruby Diamond, how it was to be inside the music—all that fireworks feeling got balled up tight in her chest until her heart felt like something fragile inside a fist.

She tugged at the knot in her shirt, pulled it down over her waist and walked over to the collection of men next to the barbeque, where the coals had withered down to a smoky red.

"Anybody got a cigarette?" Let her mother see her smoking, who cared?

"You deserve more than a cigarette," Butch said and put

his bulky arm around her. "That was something." One of the men, Charlie, she thought his name was, offered a Lucky from his pack. "Mighty fine," he said. Another man, one she didn't know, flipped his lighter open.

"Want to dance?" the man said, holding the flame to her cigarette.

He wasn't bad-looking, hair dark and combed into a wave by what smelled like her daddy's hair oil. He had a smile like some movie star whose name she couldn't think of, someone who played in a War movie.

"Sure," she said.

Louise let him put his arm around her waist; he was easy to follow. Over his shoulder she could see her mother, the cowboy's shoulders curved forward around her as they danced and her mother's fingers slowly stroking his neck. Louise put her hand against the man's neck, imitated her mother, and he pulled her closer until their bodies touched and hummed against her hair. It felt good, and maybe a little dangerous, too. She looked over at her mother whose eyes were still closed. Louise tried to close hers, too, but she couldn't keep them shut. Some irresistible pull made her keep watching her mother, her hand on the cowboy's neck. *Caressing* is the word that came to mind.

Then the song was over. She withdrew her hand from the man's, and didn't wait for him, just walked back to the line of picnic tables, to the washtub filled with soft drinks. Ice melted down so the bottles swayed in the icy water. She dove her hand in, grabbed a Coke and headed toward her tree.

"Louise." Her mother's voice loud behind her.

She turned. Her mother came toward her, her green dress flowing around her legs, her hair curled from the humidity or the dancing, her mouth set hard against all that softness.

"You better watch yourself," she said.

"You didn't like my singing?" Louise knew her voice had that tone, like when her mother said, *Don't you take that tone with me, young lady.*

"I'm not talking about your singing. I'm talking about the way you were carrying on. Dancing like that with a man old enough to be your father."

"And what about you. Dancing like that with a man who isn't my father."

The slap smacked across her face almost before the words were out, loud and stinging. Its sharp points spread up her cheek. She willed the tears to stop before they swelled. Her mother's brown eyes hardened to shells. And still the band played, and the people danced and laughed. The babble of their talk filtering through the ringing in her ears.

"Don't think you know everything about everything, Missy," her mother said. "Your father—"

"And don't you tell me about my father. He wants me to be in California."

"Well, you can't always have what you want, Louise. He should know that more than anyone."

They stood like that. The band playing, the colored lights, the party going on as if it was normal for a mother to slap her daughter's face for the first time in her life, as if a mother could just say things and do things like her daughter's feelings didn't mean anything at all.

Louise threw her Coke to the ground and pushed past her mother. It was a relief to take long strides, the straps of her sandals cutting into her heels. She crossed the patchy grass to where Butch stood with some other men. She tapped Butch on the shoulder just as The Gemstones swung into something bluesy.

"Let's dance," she said, and took Butch's hand. She led him to the center of the dusty square. Swaying her hips she turned her face up to the colored lights and the night sky beyond so whatever stars that wanted to could shine down on her.

Ruby started singing/ *Going to Kansas City/ Kansas City here I come/* slow and with a voice that sounded like she knew some things about that place.

Louise leaned close to Butch and put her hand to his thick neck. "What about it, Butch. Take me to Kansas City?" It wasn't the first time that summer she'd thought of running away.

"Any where you want to go, honey," he said.

"I mean it. I'm getting out of here and you're the man who can take me."

"You bet, kiddo. I'll just load you in my truck and drive you all the way out to California." He pushed against her waist, swinging her away in one of his unexpected twirls, the bluesy beat of the band, Lester's slide guitar twanging.

Louise swung her shoulders, hoped her mother was watching. She let Butch pull her close, his solid arm around her waist again, his hand with that stub of a finger he said got cut off in the War slipping down off her waist to the curve of her bottom. She didn't try to stop him.

"Just to Camdenton," she said. "That's not far, is it?"

She'd catch a bus; she had some money stashed, a summer long of washing dishes. She'd go to Kansas City. Get a job. Maybe as a singer. Kansas City—all those jazz joints and nightclubs. Everyone knew about Kansas City.

She leaned in close, sang in Butch's ear, *they've got some crazy little women there …/*

Butch stepped back, looked at her, beer breath warm against her cheek, the place her mother had slapped. She winked at him. What the hell.

"Take me to Camdenton, Butch, and I'll owe you one."

Paybacks

Tania Pryputniewicz

Only you'd joke through a vasectomy,
sitting up to view the clamp pinching shut
your *vas deferens* (of its lobe fished free,
fragile but firm as a bushtit's nest)
sickly white, distinct, like the diagram
they sent home between births of our second
and third child, latter nursing in my arms
while you're cauterized, next *x x* cross-stitched,
then on to bloody the left. The nurse's
shot of valium hasn't slurred your vignette
reliving the episiotomies
you watched. Naked, vitals to lamp, fear not:
you'll trump the doctor, whose post op order—
wait two days to touch the wife—you'll ignore.

What to do with Nine-Twelfths

Barbara Huntington

At the time it seemed a good idea
Dividing his ashes
One half—then another divided in sixths
For each child, his brother
And me, always trying to please everyone

But he's probably not pleased
Lurking in plastic bags, in cardboard boxes,
In the garage

Oh, one part of him is in Yosemite
Another in the surf at La Jolla
A third is in his brother's garden

But what to do with nine-twelfths?
The house?
There are already too many ghosts
Dragging their vaporous selves out from between
computers, and cell
Phones and printers and vast quantities of unlabeled
chargers

Not the vegetable garden for the confirmed hater of
spinach and broccoli!
His kids said Disneyland, but now they rarely visit
Afraid I may say,

"Just a minute, I need to give you something from the
garage."
They are wise to me
Our family of indecision, denial

So there he sits
What will I do with the nine-twelfths in the garage?

Was it Him?

Linda Hutchison

Taller than she remembers
       holding the end of
a long wooden box, lifting it
       with a younger man
at the other end into the
       back of a black truck.

His son? The last time she
       saw him he was holding
the boy. Come to tell her
       he was being sent
to fight in uncivilized
       parts of the world.

She is tempted now, shaded
       by a generation of time
to walk by, wonders if
       he would feel the burn
of her eyes.

If he would still see her
       or just a small woman
wearing black, slipping
       between pale roses
fingers open, brushing
       the bruised petals
as she passes.

When is Murder Not a Mortal Sin?

Penelope James

"It would not be a mortal sin," Great Aunt Carlota chewed her words to make them sound important, "if someone mur-der-ed that man." She patted the net on her rolled-up hair, which she never unpinned, not even at night, except for when she had it done every fortnight at the beauty parlor.

Granny drew back in horror. "God forbid, Carlota, you shouldn't say such things."

Aunt Carlota stuck up her nose and sniffed to show she didn't give a hoot. "I haven't the slightest intention of committing murder. But it is not a sin to discuss doing it." She buttered and salted half a roll and bit off the end.

We were seated around the Sunday lunch table at Granny's house in Mexico City: Grandpa from Massachusetts who'd come to Mexico forty years ago, but was still a Puritan at heart; and Aunt Carlota who watched French movies even though they were banned by the Catholic Church; and Uncle Artie who'd had a nervous problem ever since he came back from the War; and twelve-year old me and my little sister, Anne, ten, both born in England but had come to live in Mexico when my father couldn't support us. We were talking about my mother's husband Ian, a Scotsman who had turned out to be a drunken, drug-addicted, evil, crazy—as in out of his mind—stepfather.

"I do not agree," Granny said, with obvious annoyance. "Planning a murder is a sin."

"Nonsense," Grandpa spoke up. "Somebody should have got rid of the man long ago. They'd be doing the world a favor."

Aunt Carlota inclined her head toward him. "See, Amada,

Connie agrees with me."

Granny's chin shook with indignation. "If you go on like this, I'll leave the table."

"Doesn't the way the man treats your granddaughters make you angry?"

Aunt Carlota might as well have stuck a toreador's lance in Granny's side. "Of course it does. I hate the air he breathes, but I would never dream of murdering him."

Despite her words, I knew she prayed all the time for God to deliver Mummy's soul from Ian's clutches, in whatever manner He saw fit, and if it involved Ian's death, she'd be relieved to have him out of the way.

"Why don't we change the subject?"

"I'm just trying to add spice to the conversation." Aunt Carlota shook some salt onto her chicken consomé, and squeezed a lemon slice into it, then pepper and a little chili salsa. "Conversation is an art," she said, "and it needs some pepper and salt to make it palatable, and take away the bad taste in your mouth. Now how would you go about—shall we call it—Ian's demise?"

"If we planned it like an Agatha Christie novel," I said, "that wouldn't be a sin."

Aunt Carlota's beady eyes lit up under her clotted mascara. "What a good idea. Now, tell me, which is the most important part in an Agatha Christie novel?" She clacked her teeth for emphasis.

"Who dunnit?" Uncle Artie said at once.

"The deduction process," Grandpa added.

"The motive?" I asked. "Or how the murder was solved?"

"The cover up," Aunt Carlota stated triumphantly. "It confuses the issue and allows the killer to get away—or try to—with murder." She sat back and sipped her wine.

Uncle Artie jumped in. "The point is not to find out who's guilty until the end."

"Then we'll begin with the end," Aunt Carlota said. "And work backwards from there."

"Why don't we end this discussion before it begins?" Granny sounded like a goat bleating.

"Don't people ever read the end before they get there?" Anne asked.

"You're not supposed to," I told her. "In Agatha Christie novels, the whole idea is to find out who the murderer is and put them in jail."

Aunt Carlota shook her head. "We live in Mexico, and here, people pay not to go to jail."

"But what if it's murder?"

"It depends on how much they cough up," Uncle Artie said, "but most times, it's easier to say a death was due to food poisoning or a heart attack. Less red tape for the police and more money for their cause."

"Suppose they want to do an autopsy?" I asked.

Aunt Carlota curled her lips. "Who would permit a member of their family to be butchered after they're dead?"

"What if the doctor thought it was foul play?"

"I don't know any doctor who'd argue about a corpse." Uncle Artie said.

"No doctor in his right mind would call the police." Aunt Carlota shook her head. "It would cause too many complications and compromise his reputation. Anyway, there's no time. In Mexico, a body has to be buried within twenty four hours."

"Why can't they wait a few days?" I asked.

She shuddered. "It gets disgusting. Gasses make bodies swell and decompose fast, and they stink to high heaven." Her eyebrows lifted and she wrinkled her nose. "I remember when my dear sister Clara's first husband, Pepe—may he rest in peace— passed away during the Religious Persecution, and we couldn't find a priest to bury him. You can't imagine the stink. Everyone in our house was sick to their stomachs."

She gulped and looked down at her plate and gulped again as if she was feeling like throwing up. But she continued, "Clara and I went to the jail and bribed the guards to let us in to see our cousin, the Pater, who was imprisoned for refusing to break his vows. We dressed him like a woman, and got him out that way so that poor Pepe could be buried with the proper rites." She broke off another piece of her roll.

Uncle Artie grinned. "At least you knew he was dead. Not like poor old Uncle José."

"Oh yes, we should have realized something was wrong when he didn't stink." Aunt Carlota's ample bosom jiggled with emotion. "Years after he died, we wanted to move his bones in the crypt to make room for my brother, Manuel, but they were gone. We never found out who took them."

"Do you have to go on about such unpleasant subjects?" Granny asked. "At the Sunday lunch table?"

Aunt Carlota gave her a nasty stare. "Would you prefer us to talk about domestic troubles?"

Uncle Artie said, "What makes cremation the neatest way to dispose of a body?"

Granny shook her head at him, but there was no stopping Uncle Artie and his jokes.

"You accelerate the process, ha-ha."

I laughed weakly as did everyone else except Granny. "Cremation is against the laws of God," she said.

"That can go wrong as well." Aunt Carlota had a mischievous look. How she loved stirring things up with Granny. "Remember the story about the family who made Mrs. Schultz's grandmother's ashes into soup?"

"Were they cannibals?" Anne asked.

"No, of course not." Aunt Carlota said. "They thought it was a soup package. It happened before they received the letter saying what it contained."

I was going to laugh but it caught in my throat when I saw little gray shreds floating in the chicken consomé.

"Think of all the ways you can get away with murder," Uncle Artie said. "Like the woman in the Centro who cut up her husband and stuffed him in the tamales she sold in the Zocalo. How about some tacos-a-la-Ian?"

Aunt Carlota cut him short. "We're not talking about what to do with Ian's corpse, but how to turn him into a corpse."

The maid took away the empty plates and brought in fried potatoes and a roast chicken—the kind with golden, crackly skin that they cooked on a spit and you ate with your fingers. Aunt Carlota and Anne both got a wing and a drumstick, I had a thigh, Uncle Artie and Grandpa shared the breast, and Granny always ate the Pope's Nose.

Aunt Carlota directed the maid to bring her a finger bowl with warm water, a slice of lemon and a little napkin.

I think Granny was hoping her sister had forgotten what she'd been talking about, but no such luck. "Now, where were we?" Aunt Carlota said. "Oh yes, the reason people are caught is because their motives are obvious. Therefore, beware of motives."

"Other people might have reasons to murder Ian," I said, "like revenge for what he did in the War."

Uncle Artie nodded. "Nutcases like him had a ball."

Granny gave us a murderous look. "I said enough on this subject? Why don't you tell us about the last movie you saw?"

"What could be more pleasant than discussing the make believe *murder* of someone you hate?"

"I don't see the point, Carlota."

Aunt Carlota was merciless. "If it will make you happier, Amada, we'll call the victim Mr. X. Let's say Mr. X has a bad habit: he drinks too much, or has high blood pressure and doesn't heed the doctor's warnings, or takes too many medicines or mixes them—that can lead to a stroke or kidney failure."

"What if he takes too many pills?" I asked.

Aunt Carlota scrunched up her face in delight, which made her look like a Pekingese dog. "He might take an overdose." She dipped manicured claws into a finger bowl. "The crux is that no one should suspect it was murder. A bad habit, such as alcohol, drugs, staying out late, driving too fast, can be very convenient. Because it means he could do it to himself and no one else would be to blame. Though you might have to drive him to it."

"What does that mean?"

"Give him a little hand. There are ways of pushing up blood pressure to the boiling point. Or using certain herbs or intoxicants. Too many drugs can cause an overdose. A mixture of alcohol and sleeping pills will do it every time."

"What about Seconals? Ian takes them."

She nodded eagerly. "Oh yes, they can be lethal! Lead to an overdose. Like too many Equanils. Or both."

The chicken bones had piled up on the plates, and we'd finished the salad Aunt Carlota made with her secret dressing.

"Are there times when murder wouldn't be a sin?" Anne asked.

Granny looked up and said, "Never."

Aunt Carlota said, "Amada, if someone forces someone else to commit a murder, or it is in self-defense, it would not be a mortal sin."

"Give an example," Grandpa said.

"What if you murdered a person because you were afraid that person would murder someone you love?" I asked.

"Could be extenuating circumstances," Aunt Carlota answered.

"Does that mean murder isn't always a mortal sin?" I held my breath.

Instead, Granny said, "Murderers go to Hell."

"Not if they seek forgiveness in the confessional." Aunt Carlota gave her a satisfied smile.

"In order to be absolved, they have to be truly sorry for their sins," Granny shot back. "Absolution is worthless without repentance."

"If a murderer confesses to a priest, he is absolved of his sin. Period." Aunt Carlota said.

"You're saying that a person can commit a murder and go to confession and get absolution, and get away with it?" I said.

"No, they must show true repentance," Granny answered.

"You can be sorry for offending God," Aunt Carlota said, "even if you are not sorry for what you did. There is a thin line." Like her seeing *And God Created Woman* with Brigitte Bardot despite it being on the Church's forbidden list.

"Carlota, it doesn't seem to me that you have the right attitude toward confession," Granny told her, "and please stop putting wicked ideas into Pennie's head."

The maid brought in fresh mangoes and the meringues Anne and I had bought at the French bakery.

"What do you think," I asked, "would be the penance for committing murder?"

Aunt Carlota shrugged. "Probably a novena to the Blessed Mother."

Neighboring Tones

Shannon Bates

It was Debussy we heard through the walls on our first night in the duplex at the end of Adams Avenue. We didn't dare knock on the wall or even make a noise while the music played, for fear the pianist next door would stop. We lay in bed and cuddled, sighing with each phrase so beautifully executed under the musician's fingers.

"Is that Chopin?" Nick asked me one night, while I brushed my teeth. I paused to listen, then nodded before spitting in the sink.

The move proved a beneficial change for our relationship in the beginning. I'm not sure if it was our musician neighbor or just the right time and place, but we thrived in that bed next to our musical wall. We had our own soundtrack, and the performer was nearly flawless. Impressionism and Minimalism were the norm, and this soothed our souls. But a little Beethoven was good for those passionate nights. We took our cues from the pianist's choice in scores.

Nick found out one day that a friend of ours knew our neighbor.

"I can introduce you," she offered.

"No!" Nick and I both insisted.

We didn't want to ruin the magic of the mysterious serenades. No introductions, descriptions, or even mention of a name were allowed from our friend.

"Don't even tell him or her about us," I said. "We don't want things to be weird."

On a balmy night in September, when Nick was out

enjoying drinks and live music with a new friend named Max, I was struck by our neighbor's choice to play an arrangement of Samuel Barber's Adagio for Strings. I sat alone on one hip on our bed and pressed my ear against the wall, feeling the vibrations with each chord. I hadn't heard this piece performed on piano before, but I knew every note in the climbing, yearning progression by heart. I wondered at the pianist's mood.

Whenever Nick was home, the program was similar. We heard something either pensive and calming or fervent and confident. The Barber Adagio seemed to be reserved just for me, and on multiple occasions, but only when I was alone.

It was when Nick stopped going out at night that the repertoire changed altogether. It began with Bela Bartok, which was jarring, but still enjoyable. I'm a big fan of Bartok, while Nick is not. But even I will admit that it's a strange choice just before bedtime. When we began to hear Schoenberg, I turned to Nick with a frown.

"Should we knock on the wall?" I asked with a ready fist.

"No, don't," he said. But his arms were folded tightly across his chest.

When our neighbor moved on to something only vaguely recognizable as the work of Brian Ferneyhough (because anything of his resembling tonality is questionable), I slipped out from under the covers to create a makeshift bed on the living room couch.

While Nick was at work the next day, I heard furniture being moved next door. My heart dropped at the possibility of losing the piano. I could forgive the recent musical choices. I raced outside in my pajamas to find a moving truck and two men lugging a couch across the lawn. When I asked them about the resident, one guy nodded toward the home. I went to the front door and knocked.

The woman who greeted me did so with a ragged expression on a stunning face. Her long, wavy brown hair was tangled among her arms and fingers, like ivy climbing unwelcome on a marble statue.

"You're moving out?" I asked before I was able to prepare

a calm voice.

"Ingrid," she said, and I took a step back at hearing my name. "My name is Max."

Oppressed Was Before I Was

Sylvia J. Nelson

One hundred years before my birth slavery was still a
way of life.
Historical results give way to scars reflecting their
unsavory past.
I've seen many of these realities responsible for birthing
my strife;
And darkness shadows one group of people for many
decades to last.

Hear the whip ripping into virgin flesh crying out in
desperate pain
Some defeating death, hear the broken heart strings
unable to strum
While the ground beneath holding secrets of its
undeniable red stain
My ancestors say listen, hear the truth pounding in the
distant drum.

I live in two worlds that both share me with burdens of
the unjust
Oppressed, lost in the desire of the power hungry
wanting more
Shouldering grief of many as an effort of survival
because I must
All that has not changed is because it continues as it was
before.

Product of a lifestyle that started centuries ago in lands
far away,
My ancestors lived in bondage of corruption and
incessant dismay.

Truth Is

Fred Longworth

where one contender
wrestles another
on a hard flat mat
stretched taut
and flat as prejudice permits

until by feint
by greater on lesser force
or unseen plexus jab
the one pins down the other

and where victory
so defined between the canvas
and the blue

wrings the brain of any
Johnny-in-the-grandstands
until doubt dribbles
past the popcorn and puddles
at his feet

Love Poem

Mark Tuller

I trekked up Kilimanjaro
said the nurse we met walking in the state park
it was six and a half days up
and one and a half days down

it sounded good to us, and we thought about it
but then we decided it would be more interesting

to sit in our back yard together—
me with a dark beer and you a chardonnay—
and look at the eagle that glides over the nature preserve.

Graydient

Michael Evangelista

The sky glowed orange and blue, dyed from the light of a sun lying low on the horizon. Scattered across it were cotton ball clouds, silver with a yellow trim, slowly crawling to the east.

"Beautiful, isn't it?" I took a deep breath, taking in the fresh, outdoor air. An uncommon luxury nowadays.

"I guess." Mary said. "Doesn't it get old though? I mean we come here twice a day, every day, I'm pretty sure I know exactly what the sunset and the sunrise look like by now."

"Well, since the only times we can go outdoors are during the sunrise and the sunset, you learn to appreciate it."

The sun was now a segment, shrinking by the second. Soon, we would have to go inside or risk freezing to death.

"Have you ever wondered what a full moon looks like?" Mary asked. "Or what the sun looks like when it's not sunset?"

"Not really," I replied. "One doesn't normally think of the things designed to kill them, after all."

My thermowatch beeped. The temperature already dropped from 70 degrees to 60 in less than a minute. The only remnant of the sun was a golden sliver over the edge of the planet. From the structure's PA system, an automated voice spoke. *Two minutes until automatic locks engage. All outsiders, please return to the structure interior.*

"We should go." I rose from the bench and took her hand, but Mary wouldn't budge. Instead, she looked straight up, at a deep purple sky.

"Just a little longer. Maybe we'll be lucky and we can see

a star."

Another beep. It was 50 degrees. 40 degrees. The sun had vanished. *One minute until automatic locks engage.*

"Come on, don't be ridiculous, we have to leave the balcony now," I said. I tugged at her arm. Slowly, Mary stood up, still looking overhead as I held open the station's eight-inch thick insulated door, waiting for her to step inside.

35 degrees. 30 degrees.

"Please, come inside before we get locked out."

She finally stopped looking up.

"Okay."

The station is a massive, climate controlled building 450,000 square meters in area. Accommodating, energy efficient, and completely self-sufficient, it is designed with the hopes that many generations will live and die without ever stepping foot outside of its walls. Because on a planet where temperatures fluctuate between 224 degrees Fahrenheit during the day and -315 degrees Fahrenheit at night, who would ever want to?

"What's for dinner?" I joked.

"You *know* what's for dinner," Mary said, plopping two gray plates down on the dining room table. "Meatloaf and mashed potatoes, same thing that the station gives us every Tuesday night."

"I know, I know." I took a bite of the food. "Lucky they serve this on a regular basis, huh? Meatloaf is my favorite." Mary didn't reply. She chewed blankly. A dimple appeared in the left corner of her lips. From the year or so that we've been together, I knew what that dimple meant.

"Is something wrong?" I asked.

She sighed. "No, I'm fine."

"Come on, what is it?"

Mary put her fork down. She slowly wiped her face with a gray napkin before she started.

"Don't you ever wish that we could do something different, see something new?"

"Oh no," I started. "Is this more talk about how you want to go outside past dawn or dusk?"

"No, it's not just about that. I just don't want to be stuck in this same routine anymore. I mean surely, you get tired of doing the same thing over and over again, week after week, right?"

"No, I actually don't. I like the routine, I don't know why you're so against it."

"Oh, you like the routine? So what, I'm just, I'm just crazy then, is that it, am I crazy for wanting to do something that isn't scheduled out?"

"I didn't say that."

"Then what were you saying then?"

I took a deep breath. This wasn't the first time that we had this argument. "I'm just saying, why would you want to look for something new when the usual is perfectly fine?"

"But it's not perfectly fine. I've been in this building for 22 years and it has *never* been perfectly fine."

"Okay, so what do you propose we do to make it fine again? Because—"

"I don't know what—"

"-there's plenty of things to do—"

"-I want to do, I just—"

"-in the station, we just have—"

"Will you let me talk?"

"—to look around, there's bowling, there's a buffet, there's—"

"SHUT UP!" Mary screamed. "God damn it, I can barely *stand* you anymore, you're so boring! Every fucking day, it's the same thing with you. Sunrise, eat, sunset sleep, you're not a human being any more, you're a fucking *robot*."

At some point, she had stood up from her chair. Both of her fists were planted knuckle-down on the dining room table. Somehow, her plate had found its way to the ground. It had shattered, and shards of ceramic, chunks of meatloaf, and globs of mashed potatoes now covered our dining room floor.

"So... what do you want to do differently?"

Mary exhaled. "I don't know. I just... I don't know."

She slumped down onto her chair, put her hands against her face, and started sobbing. I stood up and hugged her.

"I just want to leave this place. I hate it here."

"Honey, you know we can't do that. This station's the only place where we can survive in this entire planet. We can't leave."

"I know we can't. But I want to."

Every aspect of the station's design is a result of meticulous planning by our engineers. The station is a perfect cube in order to minimize temperature variance inside the structure and to provide a large enough surface area to be powered exclusively by its solar panels. Its internal color scheme consists of varying shades of gray due to the color's moderate heat-retentive properties. This design choice has resulted in these stations being colloquially referred to as "Graydients."

Due to the planet's extreme day and night temperatures, insulation is obviously necessary. Due to the difficulty of maintaining vacuum panels in such a large structure, layers of steel, concrete, and silica aerogel were used for insulation instead. The entire structure is also windowless in order to prevent heat transfer by radiation.

My thermowatch beeped. 60 degrees.

"Time to go, dear."

We stood up. I opened the insulated door and we both stepped inside.

"I knew you'd get used to the routine sooner or later. Isn't it nice doing things regularly?"

Mary nodded as I closed the door behind us. An automated voice on the PA spoke while we walked down the exit hallway. *Two minutes until automatic locks engage. All outsiders, please return to the structure interior.*

"So what do you think we're having for dinner tonight?" I joked. As always, she didn't react.

"Well, it's Thursday today, which probably means baked lasagna and garlic bread. I love lasagna," I said.

40 degrees.

I opened the secondary insulated door and waited for Mary to step inside. She turned to look behind her.

"Come on now, Mary, I'm already hungry. We can go outside again tomorrow to catch the sunrise."

Still, Mary stared behind her, at the balcony door. I heard

her take a few long, deep breaths. She looked around at the hallway's gray walls and the light and dark gray checkerboard pattern of tiles below our feet. Then, she turned to face me. I saw the dimple in the left corner of her lips.

35 degrees.

One minute until automatic locks engage.

Mary started running for the door.

I chased after her.

30 degrees.

She opened the balcony door.

A blast of cold air rushed into the exit hallway.

She stepped outside.

I made it to the door just as it was about to close.

45 seconds until automatic locks engage.

"What the hell are you doing, Mary?!" The frigid air rushing in practically blinded me, but through my squinting eyes, I could see her sitting down on the balcony bench.

25 degrees.

"Something different," she replied.

30 seconds until automatic locks engage.

I held the door open, hoping that she'd step back inside. "Please, come inside before you get locked out, please!"

She kept looking straight up at the bruised purple sky.

15 seconds until automatic locks engage.

"Come on, damn it, get inside! I don't want to lose you, Mary!"

20 degrees.

10 seconds until automatic locks engage.

And she saw it. A single star twinkling in a lavender sky. Though the sun had already vanished for the night, a faint band of orange light still radiated over the silhouetted skyline. Cloudless, there was nothing overhead but a single star, swimming in a sea of deep purple, sparkling for an audience of one.

Six seconds until automatic locks engage. Please stand clear of the doors.

Five.

I felt the force of the thick, eight-inch door press against my arm.

Four.

She wasn't going to move from the bench.

Three.

I stopped fighting the closing door.

Two.

"I'm sorry."

One.

Click.

I felt like I was the one that was locked out.

A Space for Smiles

Jim Moreno

What is this wonder, this writing?
This mistress of rhyme, rhythm and time
That carves a niche, a space where I can smile?
I dance with Muse and she always,
Always plays kind music, soul Salsa.

Sometimes I grow sad that it took so long
To find this lonely river,
Then I realize I am blessed
That I found her body of water at all.

Some men look for this hidden stream
All their lives and never find it.
It takes work and a keen eye to find it.
Some do but are blinded by a collective madness
for money, or wounded to apathy because
Every step is cutting pain.

Today, reciting art that I love,
Never doubting this language of mystery
will transform—
Only wondering the depth of the change—
White water? Ocean flow? Eddy?

I only know change will happen,
Like Indian Summer, like virgin spring,
Like cold wind in winter,

Like falling leaves in the moon
when elk lose their horns,
And tree bark crackles
in the numinous light of noon sun.

Solstice, Baby

Regina Morin

Sol,
you brazen, blazin' sonofabitch
you're leaving us,
splitting like a junkie shooting up
a jarfull of comets.
You're packin' up your .38 caliber
triple bolt action Uzi-pumpin'
nuclear noon,
stuffing all the stinging Purex heat you can
into the duffle bag of July,
tossing those crusty yellow lips
of a Mojave summer
into your sweaty, flame-throwing locker.
You're trailing off,
leaving a message on August's machine
about how to fake a passion of
blister-busting, sweat-stinging
hot-as-tamales-wrapped-in-Tuesday's-tabloids
summer's-ended heat.
But you're not fooling us. You're gone.
This is your last searing sigh.
You're going to meet your brother
somewhere south of here,
on the other side of the world,
share a cafe negro in Tierra del Fuego,
ease into a Barcolounger long as a shadow
on the sunset side of El Capitan.

While we're scalding our knuckles
on an overheated Chevy longbed
stuck in a rut outside of Barstow,
our trial by fire is about to expire,
your heat is depleted,
your blast is past.
You're taking off.
This is solstice, Baby!

1979

Michael W. Berns

My secretary's voice crackles through the intercom static. "There are some students here to see you; they won't say why."

"Must've been my cloning lecture—usually shakes a few up. Send' em in."

Three students, two guys and a woman, shuffle in and stand in front of my desk. The guys are wearing blue knit yarmulkes fastened to dark shaggy hair with bobby pins. The girl, who has straight black hair down to her shoulders and thick dark eyebrows, turns and gently closes the door. I recognize all of them from my intro genetics class.

We stare at each other silently for what seems like a long time, but probably is only half a minute.

"Was it the cloning lecture?" I say, as I reach for copies of my *Britannica* article, though my gut tells me this is not about class.

The girl, who apparently is in charge, says, "No professor, we're here to ask you to do something very important."

From her accent, I can tell she's Middle-Eastern.

I gesture for them to sit on the couch and chair—one of the few perks for being department head. They shake their heads and continue to stand a few feet from my desk.

"We represent a group of Israeli students. You mentioned in class that you are going to the Soviet Union to lecture at Moscow University."

"Yes, it's my third trip, why do you ask?"

"You are in a unique position to help Jews who have been

refused exit visas—to emigrate."

"I know about refuseniks; my son decried their plight in his bar mitzvah speech. But I don't know how I can help. I've been invited by the Soviet Academy of Sciences to lecture at the university. My free time will be limited, and I'll be watched."

The girl moves closer to my desk, her dark brown eyes latch onto mine. "Professor Berns, you can help Jews escape Soviet oppression."

Her comment resonates. "Look," I say, "much of my grandfather's family was wiped-out in the Odessa pogroms, and those that survived were gassed by the Nazis. My grandfather was one of the lucky ones; he was smuggled through Austria and eventually, to America."

"Then you understand the situation. We need to get our people out—you can make a difference."

All three sets of eyes are riveted on me—waiting for my answer—while I'm thinking: *this is crazy. I could be arrested.* But something inside of me is pulled toward these young people, idealists I'm sure, but pragmatists as well—they are Israeli.

I whisper, as if the walls are listening. "What are you asking me to do?"

A smile creases across her face, just for an instant. "There's a professor at UCLA who is connected with an American-Israel network. He'd like to meet you."

"You mean go to Westwood?"

"Yes, we'll give you the address and meet you there. It's not good for us to travel with you."

I'm silent while I think this over. Robbie's grandfather was very active in sponsoring Jewish emigration to the U.S. when Hitler's intentions became clear. I think she'll understand.

"Okay, can you arrange it for Saturday afternoon?"

"Yes. He said 'anytime,'" the girl answers, and turns to one of the guys, who hands her a folded sheet of paper. "Here's the address with directions. We'll be there at 2 p.m."

At home, after dinner when we're alone on our patio watching the October sun set over the Capistrano Hills, Robbie's initial reaction is blunt. "You're crazy." Then she says, "You always want to challenge the rules." Finally she says, "It's the Jewish thing, isn't it?"

"Probably. I was called "dirty Jew" in first grade, and in boarding school, the English teacher, Mr. O'Riley, teased me, and even at camp, one of the counselors made fun of my big nose. So, yeah, part of it's the 'Jewish thing.'"

"And don't forget that farmer who made you so miserable that you left after two days."

"Now, you're being sarcastic, but yes, I've been refused a lot of things for being a Jew—not getting into vet school was the big one."

"So you're going to do this?"

"I'm gonna listen."

She looks at me a long time. A glint of the disappearing sun reflects off her soft brown irises. "It's your decision, Mike. I won't tell you what to do. But I'll worry, and I still think it's crazy."

Saturday afternoon I pull into the underground garage as instructed, and park my Pinto station wagon in slot seventeen. I take the elevator to the fifth floor, find apartment 5B and push the buzzer. I notice a mezuzah mounted on the door jamb, but there's no name.

He's short; maybe five-six, wears wire-rim glasses, and is bald except for gray hair around his head at ear level. He's dressed casually, in dark slacks, and a white shirt with a slight bulge in the breast pocket. He looks to be in his sixties and introduces himself as "Sol." He gestures toward a sofa in the living room. There's expensive vases perched on stands in the entry way and corners of the spacious room. Except for a large window with drawn heavy curtains, the walls are adorned with dark wood bookcases, packed with all sorts of volumes. I hear noise down a hallway, and my three Israeli students emerge from one of the rooms. They nod in recognition and sit in chairs creating a semicircle around the sofa where I'm sitting.

On the coffee table between us there's a wide flat book that says "Israel" on the cover. On the end table there's a family picture of two adults and two teenage children. Sol is not one of the adults.

In perfect unaccented English he says, "I understand in three weeks you will make your third visit to the Soviet Union." Before I can answer he continues. "It is an important thing you will do for us."

"I'm here to listen, and then I'll decide."

The girl speaks. "You must help us. It is your duty as a Jew."

Sol, interrupts. "Sarah is fervent, but no, it is not your duty. You don't have to do anything, but if you do, the imprint on your soul will be forever."

I really don't want to discuss religion or existential philosophy, but something pulls at me; maybe it's Jewish guilt— the genetic tug of ancestors I never knew—whose lives were snuffed out prematurely.

"What are you asking me to do?"

Sol nods at one of the male students who moves down the hall toward a closed door.

He slips a small black book from his breast pocket and leans toward me. "This book-of-names contains the addresses of twenty-five refusenik families who live in Moscow. Keep it with you at all times; don't show it to anyone."

I look up as the student returns lugging a large mustard-colored faux leather suitcase. He places it on the floor next to the coffee table, unzips, and flips the top back—it's empty. Then he inserts his fingers between the bottom and the side and lifts a flap exposing a flat row of books, each one slightly larger than the palm of my hand.

"There's twenty-five prayer books plus some information about Israel, and a few recordings of Israeli folk music," Sol says, as he extends his hand with the small black book.

I reach to take it, but he holds it tight and won't release. In a throaty whisper, he says "It is important you ask each family for the names of other refuseniks." He's silent for a few seconds and then let's go.

I grasp the book-of-names. "If I agree to do this, I doubt I'll have time to visit all these families."

"Even one," Sol replies. "And you must ask for names

of other refuseniks. We pressure the U.N. and American government to force the Soviets to release our people. The larger the list of names, the more influence we have."

There's a heavy silence while I stare at the book in my hands. Thoughts rattle through my brain: *Leonid Rubin navigated a lot of Moscow red tape to get me this invitation. And Tatiana has invited me to stop at her Leningrad research institute on the way to Moscow. If I'm caught, they'll be punished.*

"I don't know," I say, as I scan the four faces intently focused on me. "What if I'm caught as I enter the country?"

Sol responds. "You're going though Leningrad. They're lax. Just look tired and bored when you pass through customs. You're a big shot professor with an invitation from powerful people; they'll pass you right through."

I peer at the four faces again, squeeze the book-of-names, and take a deep breath. "Okay, I'll do it."

That evening, standing on the patio gazing at stars, I tell Robbie about the encounter, she looks at me eyes wide, brows arched toward her hairline—further than I've ever seen them. Her voice raised a few octaves above normal, she says, "You could end up in a gulag." She turns away for a few seconds, and then faces me again. "You still have three weeks before you leave, plenty of time to change your mind." She turns and walks into the house—I continue to stare at the sky, now not sure I want to make the trip. If I cancel, other than a telegram to the Soviet Union, which is unlikely to get through, I have no way of letting Leonid or Tatiana know I'm not coming. I figure I've got a week to sort this out.

It's Friday. I'm in my office reviewing my lecture on gene therapy on human embryos, and I still haven't decided. I picture the mustard colored suitcase under an old blanket in the Pinto wagon in the university parking lot. A chill ripples through me; I grab my notes, and head to the lecture hall.

When I return from scaring the shit out of three hundred bio majors, Jack Sparks is slouched in my office sofa, feet propped on the small coffee table. I recall two years ago when he first visited me, right after my trip to Kiev. He wore a pinstripe dark gray suit, similar to the one he's in today. He handed me a business card imprinted in simple black type: "Jack Sparks." The only other information on the card was a phone number. As we shook hands he said "Central Intelligence Agency." He never said "CIA," then, or in our other meetings.

I sit in one of the chairs facing the sofa. In a monotone he says, "So, I hear you're thinking of cancelling."

I shift slightly in the chair. "How did you find out?"

He doesn't answer, just stares at me with cool slate-gray eyes.

I don't know if he knows about the Israeli plan, so I fabricate an almost-truth. "Being department chairman is more work than I imagined, especially dealing with crazy faculty—so yes—I am rethinking the trip."

Jack removes his feet from the coffee table, flexes his six-foot-plus muscular frame, and leans toward me.

"Look," he says, "we want you to make this trip. You're a distinguished professor—an expert on lasers. You won't be suspected of anything other than scientific exchange. We'd like information on the output energy of their high power lasers and the quality of the optics—especially the dielectric coatings and the sophistication of their computer interfaces."

I lean toward him. We're only a few inches apart. "So you want me to spy?" My face flushes and I feel blood pulsating in both temples.

"No—be observant—remember everything. Like your students."

"You're bullshitting me, Jack—this time you're asking for a lot more—sounds like spying. I could end up in a gulag."

He removes a pack of Camels from his inside jacket pocket, lights-up, and blows smoke in my face, just like my grandma did when she was angry. "It's not bullshit professor. You travel around the world lecturing about your innovative method of laser cell surgery, don't you?" He sends another burst of smoke at me, and continues before I respond. "You don't want to jeopardize your government grants or lose your passport, do you?"

He abruptly stands and leaves.

The next two weeks are frenzied. At home, the mustard-colored suitcase is on the pool table in the rec room, next to the hologram-generating device I helped Greg build for his high school science project. Only Robbie knows about the secret compartment. She doesn't want to look at its contents, still thinks I'm taking a big risk.

The last item I lay on top of my clothes is blue pajamas with little brown horses, my seven year-old daughter's going away gift. I zip the suitcase closed, drag it through the house to the garage, and hoist it into the raised back of the Pinto station wagon.

Robbie and I are quiet on the hour-and-half drive to the airport. I'm thinking of all the things that can go wrong. She mostly stares out the window. At LAX we hug tightly. Neither of us wants to let go. She looks at me with moist, dark brown eyes. "Send me a telegram when you get to your hotel in Leningrad—I'll be worried until I hear from you." We hug again.

Invoking the Fifth

Frank Primiano

I moved along the freezing platform with the noisy crowd, pushing to board the soot-covered, maroon Pennsy coach. Although it was after 11 p.m., people jammed the platform. I had turned up my collar and pulled down my fedora against not only the cold, but also prying eyes. The riskiest thing I could do on this job was to make eye contact.

In front of me, a woman with her head bowed under a broad-brimmed hat turned on her heels without warning. Her elbow, bent to a point as she held onto the strap of her shoulder bag, caught me just below my sternum. It found the only spot not padded by the wads of coupons and rolls of cardboard tokens in the vest under my shirt. The blow stopped me in mid-stride.

She lifted her head, and, looking into my face, said, "Beg your pardon. How clumsy of me."

She was beautiful: perfect nose, full lips, dark eyes that held mine longer than I knew was safe.

"That's okay," I said, gasping. She walked on and didn't look back. I could have watched that swaying figure all night. After an inexcusable delay, my gaze left her. Focusing on the ground with my shoulders hunched, I shuffled toward the train.

Lewis' number one rule is, *"Don't get involved with anyone or anything when you're working."* Eye contact is a sure way to get involved...and remembered. But I always had a hard time when a good-looking woman was the involvee. The trips were beyond boring without some visual diversion.

As I climbed into the car, I turned and glanced around the station. Always good to know who was behind me. I spotted the woman talking to a porter. She stood out from the crowd, not because she wore any bright, flashy colors. Just the opposite: she had on a black coat and matching hat with a white scarf draped around her neck. It was this stark black and white combination that contrasted so dramatically with the dull brown, olive drab, and khaki uniforms worn by the enlisted men and officers milling around.

My garb wasn't much better. It matched the *de facto* uniforms of grey suits, grey coats and grey hats worn by civilians. Even the dark pea coats of the occasional sailor blended into the shadows cast by the dim bulbs suspended below the concourse's dark skylights. Steam from the trains hung a milky fog in which duller colors were lost, but from which her deep black plus pure white stood out.

Ever since Pearl Harbor, transportation, especially into and out of D.C., was overcrowded. Rationing cut the availability of gas, oil, and tires for personal use. So I had to rely on trains and buses like most of my fellow citizens.

When I walked through to the last car on the train, there were, to my surprise, several empty seats. This car must have been pressed into service in a hurry because a number of the seat backs were still set opposite the direction the train was headed. I found two unoccupied pairs of seats that faced each other. I sat on the aisle looking toward the rear of the car, and placed my coat on the window seat beside me.

The jostling passengers were noisy settling in. Almost all were soldiers. Two notable exceptions were a sailor and, I assumed, his girlfriend, across the aisle two rows behind me, also facing the rear. They were stuck in a liplock, making out hot and heavy, oblivious to anyone else.

With the war on for almost three years, nearly every guy my age had either enlisted or been drafted. I thought of signing up. But my draft board sent me a letter, probably instigated by my principal, saying that, because I was a high school chemistry teacher, I had been granted a critical skills deferment. Apparently, the patriotic thing for me to do was to educate the next generation so they could help make better instruments of war.

I was safe from battle because I could teach. But that was just another way to starve. Being single, my wants weren't many. Even so, I could barely afford a room and the meals I made myself each day. Not that goods were plentiful even if I had money. But it was easier to track down a little extra butter or sugar or meat if a few spare dollars could be burned to light the way.

And what good was it that most males were overseas and women were a dime a dozen? If I didn't have a dime, I still didn't get any.

So, I took the courier job. Every Friday after school, I'd go downtown to Lewis' office, pick up a briefcase, grab dinner, and hop a train from 30th Street Station to D.C. I'd get in around ten p.m., go to the office on Connecticut Avenue, put on my loaded vest, and make it back to Union Station to catch the return train to Philly.

Inside of eight hours every week, I made triple my monthly teacher's salary. Not bad and, I convinced myself, what I did wasn't illegal. I was just a courier delivering what I was given to deliver.

I settled into the corduroy-covered seat, my briefcase tucked between me and the inside armrest. I never took chances with it in the overhead rack where anyone could snatch it. If someone did, what kind of courier would I look like without a briefcase?

My nostrils discerned a light, exotic fragrance quite different from the swirl of tobacco smoke and cleaning agents that produce the distinctive railroad coach smell. I looked up. The woman in black from the platform stood in the aisle.

"Is that taken?" She pointed to the window seat across from me.

I shook my head. She shimmied past my knees, took off her coat and hat, placed them on the aisle seat facing me, and sat.

"Oh, you're the man I bumped into getting to the train, aren't you? I must really apologize. I just wasn't looking where I was going."

Lewis was shouting in my ear, *"Remember Rule Number One: Don't get involved."*

"Don't worry about it." I said.

Her dress, as black as her coat, was a snug fit that accentuated her curves. *Why does she have to be so damned sexy?* I slid down in my seat, tipped my fedora forward over my eyes, and pretended to doze off to avoid further conversation. It was bad enough she remembered me.

Outside the train a conductor wailed, "All 'board," echoed by another one farther down the platform. A loud hiss and chug-chug reached us as the engine strained under its load. The couplers clanked, and our car jolted.

The other passengers quieted and the clatter from the tracks filled my ears. Occasionally a whistle pierced the cold night outside. The conductor collected tickets, and the lights were dimmed until the first stop: Baltimore.

Although I intended to pretend to sleep, I must have actually dozed off because the next thing I knew I was awakened by the lady in black tugging on my sleeve.

"Excuse me," she said. "Would you please watch my coat? I'll be back in a few minutes."

From beneath my hat I said, "'kay."

I remained motionless, trying to clear my head, my hat still low over my eyes. Two men in grey suits, or at least grey trousers, which were all I could see, came semi-staggering down the aisle and stopped beside me.

"Is this where she was sitting?" one guy whispered to the other.

"Yeah," was the reply.

"Do you think she spotted us?"

"No, but let's take this slow. You sit up front and I'll sit back there. Don't lose her whichever way she leaves. And no trouble on the train. Wait 'til we get to Philly."

One pair of legs walked toward the rear of the car. The footsteps of the other grey suit receded toward the front. They may have wanted to keep their conversation private, but I couldn't have heard it better if I they had been speaking right to me.

The lady in black returned carrying a cardboard cup. I remained slouched when she climbed past me to her seat. My eyes widened at the aroma of coffee that overwhelmed her subtle perfume. She said nothing, but sipped while gazing into the blackness outside.

I'm a sucker for a pretty face; I stared at her profile. But no way was I going to warn her and draw attention to myself. She looked calm, alert. Not once did I see her lids droop.

Nothing happened during the stop in Baltimore. However, as we pulled out of the station at Wilmington, the conductor waddled up to my seat and leaned in front of me toward the lady in black. In a stage whisper he asked, "Ma'am, are you Miss Hurley?"

Her answer was a hesitant but audible, "Yes."

"A man in the station asked me to give you this." He reached forward and grasped her hand. When he released it she held a folded piece of paper that had been pressed into her palm. The conductor walked away.

A scowl crossed the woman's face. She unfolded the paper on her lap and read it before tearing it, over and over. She put the pieces in her purse.

Her body tensed as she raised her head and scanned the front of the car. Feigning a yawn, she covered her mouth and turned to view the rear seats. Before facing front again, she shuddered with what must have been the shock of recognition. Her hands clutched her bag, kneading it like bread dough as she stared ahead.

"Philadelphia...Thirtieth   Street   Station...three minutes...all those getting off in Philadelphia gather your belongings...Philadelphia..." the conductor announced.

I sat up. The lights in the car brightened. People rustled from sleep, put on coats, and moved suitcases into the aisle. Across from me Miss Hurley was also busy. She had produced a parcel the size of a paperback book from somewhere. Although she tried to shield her actions with her bag, I saw her wedge the package between her seat cushion and the side of the car. When she stood to leave, no signs of it were visible.

I pictured Lewis sitting behind his desk pontificating, *"Rule Number Two: Never get caught with the stuff on you. Ditch it if there's any chance you'll get picked up, or, worse yet, hijacked."* Miss Hurley, or her boss, must have subscribed to that same philosophy.

Wearing her hat but carrying her coat, she pushed to the front of the car. I turned my head to watch her bump into people as the train shifted and rocked on the turns leading into the station. But drooling over her wiggling backside was a luxury I couldn't afford right then. I reached across the seat she had vacated, retrieved the parcel and slipped it inside my overcoat which I grabbed in the same motion.

The grey suit from the rear muscled his way through the car's crowded aisle. When he came abreast of me he stopped and grunted a "'Scuse me" as he bent over my knees. He looked at, under, over and around the seat that the woman had occupied. Growling something I couldn't understand, he continued to where his partner sat, both of them waiting behind the lady in black.

My briefcase lay flat on my lap. Up ahead, the grey suits were eyeing Miss Hurley. I eased the package into my briefcase.

"Rule Number Two," Lewis was shouting, *"Never get caught with the stuff on you."*

The train glided to a controlled stop. Steam hissed below the windows. A mad rush broke from the doors. The woman disappeared into the crowd. The grey suits plunged in after her.

I let the aisle clear and then stood up. The sailor and his girlfriend were asleep amid all the commotion. She was in his lap and they were still joined at the mouth. He was keeping his right hand warm inside her blouse. I couldn't help feeling a little envy.

I stepped from the train. The platform bustled with activity as it had in Washington. I climbed the stairs to the station's street level amongst a contingent of marines. As I strode through the gigantic marble cavern, I scanned the crowd for anyone paying too much attention to me, the way Lewis said to do. I saw no lady in black, and no followers in grey suits. They had evaporated.

I left the station, walked past the line of taxis engulfed by the arriving passengers, through the lighted parking area, across Market Street toward 31st and into the chill morning darkness.

I passed the grain elevators beside the trestle over Market Street leading to the rail yard behind the station. A green and silver Speedy Cab turned east onto Market and approached me.

Before I became a courier, I had wondered why there was never a shortage of taxis. They were everywhere. Rationing must have hit taxi companies like everyone else. So my question had been, "Where did they get their cars, tires and gas and oil?"

Speedy Cab was a prime example. It had been a two-car operation when the war started. But now it had a fleet second only to Yellow Cab. It was a remarkable success story that made its owner, Big Eddie Granito, rich.

I hailed the cab and got in. The driver and I exchanged greetings and we took off toward center city.

This was the part that baffled me. Why couldn't I just go home when I got back to town? No, there was a procedure, one of Lewis' unnumbered rules: "Let the cab drop you near the office no matter what time it is, like you were goin' there to finish your business. Go in, turn on the lights, put the briefcase in the filing cabinet, hang around a couple minutes, then leave."

His damned paranoia. Who's watching anyway? Procedures, procedures, rules, rules.

As the cab crossed over the Schuylkill, I began another of Lewis' procedures that I had executed many times. I opened my overcoat and jacket, and unbuttoned my shirt. I reached inside and undid the snaps that released the vest I wore in place of an undershirt. I pulled the vest and its straps out through the front of my shirt making sure that nothing fell from the fourteen pockets sewn into it. I folded it and stuffed it under the driver's seat. I buttoned up, rearranged my tie and coat, and sat back.

"Thanks, kid," the cabbie said.

I still had a few minutes. Now was my chance to examine the package. Holding my briefcase so the driver couldn't see it in the rear view mirror, I raised its flap. The package was mixed in with the legal papers I carried as decoys. Without removing it from the briefcase, I unwrapped one end exposing several paper-covered rolls about the diameter of a dime. I took one out. The end was open but curled around the edge to retain its contents that were red cardboard discs embossed with a "D."

Ration tokens like the ones I'm carrying. From the size of the package there must have been two, three thousand dollars worth, maybe more, if they were sold to a fleet operator like Granito. My imagination took off. *Lewis and I can be rich. This can be the nest egg we need to set up our own coupon exchange instead of just running them around for the dealers.*

Rules, rules, rules…Lewis, again, shouting in my ears, *"Rule Number Three: Never get greedy…understand? It don't pay in the long run."* What to do?

The cab stopped a block from the office. As I got out, the driver said, "Bye, kid. Take care a yerself."

"You too, Big Eddie."

I climbed to the second floor office. A lamp inside backlit the lettering on the door: "Ives Courier Service, G. David Lewis, Regional Manager."

I used my key. Lewis looked up from the only desk. A stratified haze rose from his perpetually-lit Camel, layering the upper third of the room.

"Well, how'd it go?" he asked. He removed a tobacco speck from his tongue, rolled it around between his thumb and middle finger, then flicked it away.

"Funny you should ask."

"What the hell does that mean?"

I sat in the chair in front of the desk and spent the next ten minutes telling him the story right up to my dilemma in the green and silver cab.

"You ass hole," he said. "Don't you remember the rules? I didn't make them up for nothing. Not only were you already at risk by having our stuff on you, you go and get greedy and get more that's not even hidden." He sucked on the cigarette and exhaled.

"Well, at least you didn't try and go out on your own. Your tail would a really been hangin' out then." He lit a new cigarette from the one he held. "So, let's see the stuff."

"Don't have it."

"What?"

"Your rules must have sunk in, or maybe your paranoia. I don't know. I decided perhaps I shouldn't get greedy. So now Big Eddie has a present he wasn't expecting. Could be, one day he'll throw some extra business our way to return the favor."

Lewis looked at me and gritted his teeth. "I'm makin' up Rule Number Four right now," he said. "Rule Number Four: Don't be stupid. Never give anything away for free."

"I thought about that. But I figured what if this is a setup? It was just too easy. It was like she wanted me to have the stuff, and those two guys were putting on a show for me. And what was with her goring me with her elbow? I think she was trying to find out if I had my vest on."

"Real-ly?" Lewis frowned, emphasizing the first syllable of the word. "Are you sure she didn't just want to look into those dreamy eyes of yours?"

"Yeah, maybe she wanted to be sure it was me. But she still couldn't frisk me. So an accidental collision gave her a one-shot chance to feel if I were armor plated…and she hit my soft underbelly which didn't tell her what she wanted to know. That meant she had to plant something on me if they wanted to nail us."

"Man, you're in fantasy land. You need some sleep."

"You're right. I was too tired to think straight. I just kept getting more confused. So I decided, to hell with it. We aren't countin' on this stuff, so no big loss."

Lewis said, "Ya know? I got rules so you don't need to think…Damn…Goodbye, Easy Street." He coughed on the next drag. "You keep any souvenirs? Maybe a roll or two?"

"Nope, it's all in the cab."

More gritting of teeth. "You just better remember Rule Number Four from now on. Understand?"

As if in answer to the question, a loud knock rattled the office door. I jumped. Lewis glared at me, then at the door. I rose, walked in no hurry across the room, and turned the knob.

In the hall, standing at military-style attention, holding silver badges in their left hands, were the sailor and his lipmate from the train. In the sailor's right hand was a sheaf of papers with "Search Warrant" printed across the top.

"I think you have something you shouldn't," he said.

Ignoring him, I turned to Lewis and said, "Rule Number Five: Screw Rule Number Four."

Pure Seduction

Claudia Poquoc

The Oh, Oh, Oh's in Koto music
make these vibrant strings sing.
They pluck my harp of stone
divining it a pair of wings.
I tremble with its undertones
my rising waters humming
drawing up unnatural sounds
that lovemaking can only dream of
without these flawless fingerings
without these waves of unearthly strings
that rise from an underground torrent
then flood my shuddering shore.

Rosemary in Olive Oil

Anne Canter

Rosemary leaves a wild, witchy scent on
my fingers as I drop the needles into
sizzling olive oil, humming some Simon
and Garfunkel, while memories of the field
of rosemary behind the house where my boyfriend
first said "I love you" rise with the smell of supper.
That was back when he cooked for me
and not the other way round.

Now he comes to our table, and I set
a bowl before him, hope and desperation steaming
from the penne and white beans.
"I worry you won't like it," I say to fill
the silence, take my own bite.
It leaves a bitter flavor on my tongue.

A Poem for D.

Anitra Carol Smith

I thought you were a boulder,

Insouciant and immutable.

But you were a blossom

Nodding on a stalk

Like the rest of us,

Your time cut even shorter

By a tentative heart

With a limited warranty.

A Danger to the Family

Chloe Sparacino

AUGUST 14, 2010

I tell myself I am doing the best I can in the moment as I lie on the hard as a board carpeted floor of my studio apartment listening to the sound of restlessness creeping across my skin. This morning has stretched open into a hot and sunny Saturday, and I am too comfortable wearing my pajamas to change out of them, but I do not want to stay cooped up inside my apartment either. My orange and gold curtains from Pier One waltz over the wind of my open windows as I inhale the scent of dusty air, fresh sun, and new adventures.

Hopping on my sister Jemima's bicycle—she lent it to me indefinitely when I moved to San Diego last year because she never uses it—I ride downtown in my pajamas, from Hillcrest to Petco Park and the Convention Center, back through the Gaslamp district, and then to Little Italy for a snack. Downtown is full of weirdoes and I am welcomed into their family as I fly by at ludicrous-speed.

"Hey girl, keep smiling!" Homeless men look up from their overloaded shopping carts to call after me.

On my way home through Little Italy, humanity is climbing out of bed at noon and sleep-walking outside for coffee. I lock up my bike and join the line. Right before I order coffee at Café Italia, I make sure I have enough cash tucked into my shoe because they only take cash, and I make sure to wait next to the gelato counter because that is how the line works at this café. The gelato is so good if they did not put the glass cover over top, all the customers would dive their heads right into the cold creamy tubs and make a huge mess.

I bounce with excitement thinking about how I will be spending the rest of the day with my niece and nephew, Hanna and Theo, and I know we will pretend something, indulge in something, and create something, and I have no idea what any of it will be but I cannot wait to find out.

OCTOBER 16, 2010

At any moment, any time during the day, I think about Hanna and Theo and start crying. Strangers smile apologetically at me because my pain walks before me like my own personal assassin. Shrapnel from my broken heart flies around me and stings my shocked face. I do not want to fall asleep because every day that goes by is one more day further away from everything that was home.

I cannot stop these spontaneous combustions of grief and tears. Losing my family has left me feeling empty and alone. The worst part is that my niece and nephew have been told I want nothing to do with them. I need to start writing down my Hanna and Theo memories so I do not forget them, so one day, decades from today, they might try to contact me and I can show them the memories I remembered to keep. They will be all I have because I might not be getting any future memories.

AUGUST 14, 2010

After I bike home, I shower and dress and drive to my sister's house to babysit. My eight-year-old niece and four-year-old nephew ask if we can visit The Marston House in Balboa Park, one of the first craftsman houses built in the United States. They have been to the Marston House before with my sister Jemima, but they want to go again and take me on the tour. During the hour and a half walk through the old house, they eat up every word the tour guide says and we pretend we live there. Hanna and Theo show me where they would sleep, and where I would cook our meals, and then we walk around on the trails behind the house and discover a wedding in the garden. We hide behind the bushes to spy for a while.

OCTOBER 16, 2010

Hanna and I used to make-believe playing "house" and would cook "dinner" using the miniature plastic kitchen Jemima set up in her dining room, and we would pretend the kitchen caught on fire. As we screamed for help, Theo would march in wearing his rain boots, carrying a rope as a pretend hose, to rescue us and put out the fire.

AUGUST 14, 2010

I drive Hanna and Theo back to my studio apartment and we wash our feet in my bathtub because somehow we got filthy creeping through the bushes of Balboa Park. Hanna and Theo play with the stuffed animals and Playmobil school bus I keep for them in my apartment, and they hide in my closet giggling while I make quesadillas in the toaster oven. We sit around the kitchen table and eat dinner, fully enjoying this sacred moment of eating with our hands, while Theo eyes my bike suspiciously because he does not appear to believe a kitchen is where a person should store their bike. We get in the car as the day is starting to get dark and drive down the street to Fiji Yogurt to try some samples. I make us three small sundaes of chocolate raspberry frozen yogurt to indulge in.

"How do you know how the yogurt machines work?" Hanna peers up at me from behind her soft brown hair.

"I learned by watching other people do it," I tell her, and I can see her young mind storing this piece of wisdom somewhere safe and accessible behind her big brown eyes.

I did not think we created anything because we ran out of time, but Hanna reminds me as I am writing in my journal that we created the best chicken quesadilla the three of us have ever tasted, except Theo picked the chicken out of the cheese because he prefers it plain.

Back in the car, the kids put on their slippers and hug their stuffed animals and we drive the thirty minutes back to their house for bedtime, and they are way too excited to fall asleep in the car because of the sugar from the yogurt and because of all the fun we had. At home, after they brush their teeth and put on their pajamas, we read bedtime stories sitting crammed up together like one person with three heads and six arms in the oversized purple chair in their living room. There is no way they get to bed on time.

OCTOBER 15, 2010

I am sitting in my grey car in a grey parking, about to meet Jemima's husband Ben for lunch at the Miami Grille near his office in La Jolla, and I do not know what is going to happen. I need to prepare myself and go in with very low expectations. I do not owe him anything but I can love him, although I am not sure what love looks like right now. Ben emailed me wanting to meet for lunch because he has designated himself as the spokesperson to go between me and the rest of my family.

I have not seen Hanna and Theo since the day I took them to the Marston House in Balboa Park. I have been having nightmare memories about being sexually abused by my mother, in the nursery of my past with dark corners and red rage, and I do not know what to believe or who to trust anymore, because the memories feel real and make sense to me. I am afraid to call my sister and hear her tell me I am crazy. My family knows my maternal grandmother sexually abused me when I was eight years old—she was mentally unstable and very depressed, and also abused my uncle when he was a child—but abusive flashbacks of my mother stretch the reality of my mind into the edges of insanity, begging the question, "What am I supposed to do with this?"

I wrote out my nightmare memories and emailed them to my brother Eliab in Canada, and Jemima in San Diego, in an effort to make sense of what I saw inside my mind. I also posted the dark memories on my blog, which approximately five hundred people from my family's church community reads, because the attendees of my sexual abuse support group keep saying, "If only I had warned everyone about my abuser. Then maybe the rest of my family would not have been abused the way I was." When she saw my blog, my mother called me right away but I did not pick up the phone. I can barely think about her without shaking all over. I am terrified to ever see her or speak to her again, terrified of how readily I give her control over my thoughts and emotions when I talk to her.

In the dismal parking lot of the Miami Grille, I write myself a letter from my inner child: *Dear Chloe, You are about to meet with Ben and find out where you stand with the old family and soon you will learn what your new family will look like but until then what I need is for you to sit up straight and smile and relax and be honest about your sexuality and tell yourself you are incredibly brave and beautiful. I love you. Love, Little Chloe.*

OCTOBER 16, 2010

One night when I was babysitting Hanna and Theo, we wrote stories together which Hanna illustrated and Theo helped me write by coming up with some of the words. We wrote a fireman story for Theo and a story about flying pets for Hanna, and we read them aloud together, over and over. I love the time I had with them, doing the things we love to do, acting out stories, drawing and writing, reading stories, while being patient with each other, working together on our projects without a care in the world. Those are the best kind of memories.

OCTOBER 15, 2010

Once I finish exactly half my steak salad, Ben tells me that he and Jemima are not giving Hanna and Theo the funny stories and cards I have been sending them in the mail. I put my hand over my chest and inhale sharply through my mouth. They have told the kids that I am taking a break from the family.

I do not want to take a break from Hanna and Theo, but Ben says by publicly discussing these private issues, my recovery from sexual abuse on my blog, I have betrayed their trust. He does not believe me, and he thinks I am projecting the abuse from my grandmother onto my mother. He says I am dangerous because of what I am saying about my mother, and he has to protect his family. He does not want me tainting his children's view of their grandmother.

My number one job is to live authentically, and so I

have decided that today is the day I follow my heart and lose my family in the process. I drive back to work after lunch and collapse, sobbing uncontrollably, in the arms of Marycruz the cleaning lady. She does not understand English very well so she takes me outside and points to the enormous blue sky and tells me to be grateful and thank God for all his blessings. The sky looks smaller than the giant hole of sadness that is forming inside my heart.

OCTOBER 16, 2010

One Saturday for lunch, I took Hanna and Theo to the Corvette Diner and when Theo ordered a hotdog, the wait staff sang him "The Weenie Song" which the three of us thought was weird and embarrassing, but we laughed about it later. Then Hanna and Theo wanted to take their dad there for Father's Day so the five of us went and Theo ordered a hotdog again and they sang "The Weenie Song" again. He did not eat much hotdog both times, but the kids did get balloon hats made for them with spirals and colors and bouncy springy-things, like exclamation points leaping off their heads.

OCTOBER 15, 2010

After I get home from work, I lay down on my back on the apartment floor wondering what to do, and then I leap up and load my car with Jemima's bike, helmet, and the bike pump Ben had lent me. I get the bike in my car by taking off the front wheel, and I drive up to their house at 7:30 p.m. and ring my sister's doorbell. Ben sees me in the peep hole of their yellow front door, and I hear him sending his kids to the back of the house with Jemima. He comes outside and stands on his front porch, blocking me from the front door.

"You cannot come inside because I need to protect my wife and children. You are a danger to my family, and you are disrespecting us by showing up here," Ben says.

"I want to say goodbye to my sister and the kids," I tell him.

"No, it is too confusing for the kids, and I do not want

you tainting their relationship with their Nana."

My hands are shaking so I hug my chest and take a step back from their front porch. He has packed my heart with dynamite and blown out an empty cavity.

"I needed to hear that from you, that this is where you stand, I needed this dose of reality. But I came to say goodbye to my sister and the kids. I miss them so much."

Ben hesitates, thinking before speaking. "I can't risk you talking to the kids. What are you going to do, say goodbye to them for two weeks, two months, forever? They won't understand. You coming over tonight disrespects us all," he raises his voice and stands firm.

"Well you are disrespecting me because you refuse to believe me," I reply. Ben leans back and the weight of this conversation is almost too heavy to carry. I turn away because my whole body starts sobbing.

"I can put myself in your shoes and understand, but this hurts so bad, my heart is breaking. I cried all day today. This is the worst kind of pain," I exclaim, and Ben's demeanor softens a little. He follows me to my car and asks if I need help getting the bike out. I hand him the skeleton of my sister's bike, the front tire, and the bike pump.

"This is worse than Grandma…and everything," I tell him as I climb into my car sobbing. As I drive away, strangely I feel better, because I stood up for myself, I was authentic with my feelings, and I fought the battle of my life. I have fought for something I love and it was not a loud, messy, or brutal fight, but a strong, beautiful outcry of pain.

OCTOBER 16, 2010

Hanna liked to exclaim, "Aunt Chloe you are SO CRAZY!" and I know she loved that about me. I would ask her, "Why am I SO CRAZY? I am perfectly normal." Then I would do a little dance and make a kooky face, and she would laugh and imitate me.

One time when I was babysitting, all Theo wanted to eat was granola. He kept saying "nola" whenever I asked him what he wanted to eat—for breakfast, lunch, and dinner. Hanna and I could not stop laughing every time he said "nola" which only made him smile and say it more.

OCTOBER 21, 2010

I receive a FedEx envelope at work today—an overnighted, handwritten, two page letter from my brother Eliab in Canada. He writes he cannot go on this journey with me and he does not believe my mother-abuse memories. I shove the letter in the back of my closet and refuse to read it ever again.

I wonder if this massive hole in my heart will ever stop aching. Focusing on the loss of Hanna and Theo helps me shelve the intense mother loss I am feeling. I am starting to have dreams about my niece and nephew, but if my mother appears in a dream I wake myself up, drowning in sweat and fear, before I can see what happens next. Sometimes Hanna talks to me in the dreams and tells me she understands and she and Theo still love me. Other times they look sad, scared and alone, and refuse to speak to me. I wake up crying from these dreams but I will not waver from my path. I am seeking an authentic, true life because I want to discover the truth about my family at any cost.

I have been reading *Lit* by Mary Karr because my writing professor friend told me I would be able to relate to her journey. The first half of the book made me terribly thirsty for beer, and I wanted to get drunk just like she was getting drunk all the time in the book, but I am reading the last half now where she is in a twelve-step program, so it is getting easier to read. I am going back to therapy just to have someone to talk to because my phone does not ring anymore since my family and I are estranged. I have started puking up quesadillas at home, and staring off into space at work, but I feel a strength building inside me—if I can get through this, I could survive just about anything.

OCTOBER 16, 2010

I think Hanna and Theo hung the moon but I have to let the kids go—they are not mine—and this must be what adults feel like when they wish they had spent more time with their children but now it is too late. I did the best I could at the moment and I cannot go back in time and change what happened, but I can continue to follow the guidance of my inner wisdom and see where she leads me. I will make mistakes, yes, but I know there is always more for me to learn, more sky for the heart to swallow, and a new adventure waiting to be discovered.

Aging Achers

Lawrence Richard Carleton

W ell, today was the big art and lit show here at Aging Achers. You weren't there, my darling daughter, but then I didn't expect you. I went after all, but I didn't contribute anything. You know my attitude toward these things: it isn't an exercise in people who happen to be old contributing to the Great American Conversation; it's "oh look these old coots are keeping themselves busy, let's give them some attention before we slide it all down the memory hole." It's too bad, too, 'cause some of the stuff was pretty original. I liked Daisy Friendly's life sized statue of George Dubya Bush with bullhorn. She went to the zoo and brought back a huge supply of paper made from elephant dung and created the statue entirely from that and chicken wire. She must've spent a fortune! The zoo just sells the stuff in small souvenir packages, and she would've had to buy a lot of them. At the short story session Big Al Knudson came through with a side-splitter about his old job covering up leaks in the Keystone Pipeline in Canada.

Channel Five covered the event, in a manner of speaking. Did you see it? If you did you know what I mean. A quick pan of the hall mostly showing old people sitting in chairs, instead of the art they produced, a few seconds of Al reading his story—not enough to get a sense of it—and inane interviews with random attendees about how it was good to keep busy when you're old. The only art that got much attention in that report was Mrs. Wall's wall of art, which consisted of her copies of twentieth century masterpieces.

I tried to get interviewed to make a statement about how

some of these people have something worth seeing or hearing to offer, but apparently I looked too conscious to fit the story the news team was looking for. Anyway following the reporter all over the place got me nothing but dirty looks.

After that I snuck out to the Limbo Bar—"How low can you go?"—to catch up on sports in peace and quiet.

I know you wanted me to read one of my stories at the show. (Would you have come?) Better than nothing, you say, given my lack of any publications through years of writing. Well, some of my stuff has been published, kind of, though not in a way to make a name for myself. I'll explain.

Remember I snagged a gig as a volunteer at *Dissonant Voices Online*? I know I've said you ought to check it out. Well, my job there is to read and recommend online contributions. Most of it is the usual stuff about unemployed dropouts having problems with beer and sex, but occasionally there's something about intelligent people dealing with some issue which matters. (I'm going to try to get Big Al to send us his story.) Anyway, one day last year I got a manuscript titled "Mary Hale," about a girl who gets pregnant without having sex (though she's not a virgin) and gives birth on Christmas Day. Much discussion of religion ensues. This story was particularly interesting to me, since it was word for word what *Crab Pot Quarterly* had rejected when I sent it to them earlier that year. The putative author of this questionable submission was one Billy Bockfuss. Billy Bockfuss! Who was he kidding? Did he think no one would recognize the name as a character from John Barth's *Giles Goat-Boy*? Yet when I checked, there he was on the web: William "Billy" Bockfuss, an up and coming academic who works on the editorial board of—surprise—*Crab Pot Quarterly*. What to do? Claim plagiarism? Then the story—one of my best—would never get published. I decided to recommend that we publish it. At least I would know that one of my works made it to print.

That wasn't the end of it. "Mary Hale" got more hits than anything else we'd ever put online, and was an easy choice for lead story in our print anthology that year. So at least now you know I can write.

I began to think maybe I was on to something. My "Parker's Progress" hadn't found a home, and I'd sent it to a huge number of magazines, but not *Crab Pot Quarterly*. It's a pretty good tale of a disgraced minister—actually the one responsible for Mary Hale not being a virgin in the other story—who quite by accident finds himself elected to the Michigan legislature and confronted there with the ethical dilemma posed by horizontal fracturing for natural gas: accept badly needed money from the industry or stand up for the environment. I sent that off to *Crab Pot Quarterly*, which quickly rejected it. Then a few weeks later there it was, submitted to *Dissonant Voices Online* by the same Billy Bockfuss and assigned to me for evaluation. Of course I approved, we published it, and it was as popular as "Mary Hale."

Well, those stories actually were the first two parts of a short story trilogy I'd written before I moved in here. Put together, they bring attention to my three main concerns: religion, environment, and politics.

Naturally I proceeded to try my luck with my third story, "Welcome Home." In this one a guy who went off to the Iraq invasion thinking he was defending America learns, event by event, that the operation really was an unprovoked war of aggression against a country everyone should have known had nothing to do with 9-11 and was no threat to the U.S. He returns from his tour of duty and is treated like a hero when he knows he's really participated in a moral offense. Then a TV station schedules a series of interviews with vets. He tells his story. Later, he watches the resulting broadcast, titled "America's Heroic Defenders." Hero after hero recounts his tale of danger and daring, peppered with patriotic statements. The show ends with the acknowledgement that "these are just some of the defenders of freedom we interviewed," and a quick flash of pictures and names, including his. "Thank you every one of you," the narrator concludes, "for defending America's freedom."

I sent in "Welcome Home" to good ol' *Crab Pot*, got the expected rejection, and waited for the next offering from Billy Bockfuss. In a few weeks, there it was, but the end was different! This time the guy's interview is presented, but edited to sound confused and incoherent, with the narrator summarizing it with the suggestion that some returnees suffer from post-traumatic stress disorder. What could I do—complain that Mr. Bockfuss hadn't done an honest job of plagiarism? I recommended we respond with a request for rewrite: wouldn't it be more realistic, I suggested, for the guy's statement of the truth to go ignored, instead of the reporter dishonestly mischaracterizing him as unbalanced? Unfortunately the other reviewer asserted that we should respect the authorial integrity instead of trying to redo Bockfuss's work the way we would have written it—especially since Mr. Bockfuss has shown himself to be such a unique and original voice!

So there it is, in our current issue: my antiwar masterpiece hijacked by an untrustworthy plagiarist. (You should read it anyway, and the other two, now that I've identified them.)

Oh, it may occur to you on learning the contents of my stories that I'm kind of airing family laundry. Your mother worried about that when I started writing. I promised her that I'd never do that, and I think I've kept my word.

For example, you're not "Mary Hale." You never identified the father (though I had my suspicions), but you didn't deny there was one, and anyway you never had the baby.

As for the second story, your Uncle James is not the Reverend Parker. Your uncle did campaign on an anti-fracking platform, but in his case, as you know, he got outspent and didn't come close to getting elected.

And of course your brother saw through the lies by the time they shipped him off to Iraq. We don't know what he would have said had he made it back.

So these stories are really the result of my imagination running away, playing "what if."

Which brings me to one reason it's good I moved into this old folks home after your Mom died, and turned over the house to you and your life partner. (By the way, now that it's legal, maybe you and she can get married. Nudge nudge...)

I've had it with Billy Goat-Boy Bockfuss. I have a new masterpiece to get into print, and this time I'm going to be my own middleman. I've sent this latest item in my oeuvre directly to *Dissonant Voices* as Ebenezer "Ben" Cooke. (I'm a John Barth fan too, so I appropriated the main character from *The Sot-Weed Factor*. "Henry Burlingame" has been done, but I don't think "Ben Cooke" has.)

You're going to like "The Monty Banks Collection." Guy Ernest tells the story: Monty is a notorious art dealer, known for important "finds" of dubious provenance—Mondrians, Giacomettis, Pollocks—works unknown until "discovered" by Monty. He's also a philanthropist, specializing in advocacy for the aging. When his sister Muriel Banks Otis dies at Ancient Acres Homes for Active Seniors he retires, and shortly after shuffles off this mortal coil himself. He leaves a generous donation to the city art museum, on condition that they install a special wing for his private collection. Of course they accept the donation, and with it the collection, sight unseen. When the wing is created Monty's designated executor—Muriel's son Jeff—hauls the works from Monty's home and installs them in the museum, all under the greatest secrecy. After much anticipation, the grand opening occurs with great fanfare. The crowd of dignitaries files in, emitting oohs and ahs as they stroll past one masterpiece after another, all by previously unknown artists. The occasion is a wild success. It's only much later, when curiosity leads aficionados and reporters to track down these newly discovered painters and sculptors, that it's revealed that they all were Muriel's friends at her retirement home.

Guy Ernest is a bit curious, though, and eventually on one of his visits to the museum he spies Muriel's son there and collars him for a chat. Guy, after all, is from the same old folks home as Muriel and though he didn't know her very well, he does remember that she was supposed to be a pretty good artist herself.

"Why isn't any of Muriel's work in the show?" he wants to know.

"Mom's work is in museums and private collections all over the world," Jeff replies with a wink. "She doesn't need exposure."

Pretty good story, eh?

Where *did* I come up with the idea for it?

Anyway, I set up a fake email account for bencooke@ fastfastfast.com, but I needed a residential address. So, if you get anything in the snail mail for the aforementioned Mr. Cooke, kindly notify me. Maybe you could visit your old Dad some day here at the House of Undignified Decay and bring it along with you.

Now I'd better hit the Send button so I can head out to The Dubious Dive and drink like the fishes.

Dang, there's the nurse with my nightly meds. She's not just leaving them either. She's going to sit there until she sees me take them. Must not be a busy night. Maybe when you come you can have a talk with them about this.

Anyway, I'm signing off now. Hope to see you soon!

Love,

Dad

The End of the World Cometh

Mary Fry

"I know the exact date the world will end." I looked up from my computer. I was trying to write at a local coffee house in San Diego. An older man with a bucket and a squeegee sauntered over, smiling, as if the end of the world was something to look forward to. I had a dream years ago, a glowing rock hurling down from the sky, staring at it with terror and fascination. Now I always pay attention when there is a report that an asteroid is whizzing by. I never used to hear about them. Now they are coming closer and closer, faster and faster. It's a bad omen. Obama seems to be concerned. He wants to blast them out of the sky. He's as nervous as me.

I grew up always afraid of such things. I was very gullible. California was supposed to fall into the ocean on this one particular day when I was 10. I was petrified, standing there by a little league field in Carmel, my heart beating wildly, the radio was casually playing "someone left the cake out in the rain, and I don't think I can take it because it took so long to bake it and I'll never see that cake again." Who cares about that damn cake! I waited. It was the eve of destruction. California in its neat bent elbow shape was going to shear off into that big water, just a mile or so from here. And yet, if it floated so nicely away, that would be okay. There still would be Seven Eleven stores and blue raspberry slurpies. But if there was a huge splash, well, you just didn't know how you would come out.

The other problem about California was earthquakes. "The Big One." When that rumbling began, when would it ever end? I was in the Palo Alto when the Loma Prieta earthquake hit. It started so gently as I typed in my cubicle, and I wasn't fazed because in a minute I knew all would calm down. But no, it jolted and bucked and I flew under my desk as the ceiling tiles tell down and snakes of black wiring sparked and slapped the floor. There was a scream "It's the big one!" It was big, just not The Big One. But it gave me a taste of Armageddon. The exploding transformers, all the windows in my 1920's garret shattered. Outside the wail of sirens in the dark. Neighbors who never said hello gathered around a radio. Someone ordered pizza before the quake, so we all shared it. A wealthy looking old lady came by, she had no food. She joined our circle and sat on the steps nibbling a pizza crust. Disaster was a great leveler.

My dad was always talking about sheep when it came to the end of the world. The good sheep versus the bad ones. How could you tell a bad sheep from a good one anyway? Did they just look more guilty? And yet they would be separated, the good from the bad, the wheat from the chaff. The good sheep baaing and cavorting, the good life in the clouds. And those bad sheep wandering around in the caves of hell, their lips lucky to find a tuft of moss.

The man who just told me about the end of the world stood in front of me now blocking the sun. "It's proven, the world will end in October, you'll see." I thanked him of informing me of my untimely death. He ran off to rescue his car meter, came back. "So another word of advice," he offered leaning on his squeegee. "Quinoa, put it in the crock pot. Steam your vegetables. And eat sausage. You need fat. And," he said with a pregnant pause, "a teaspoon of borax in distilled water, daily. Cures all your ills. That's how Alexander Graham Bell recovered from a serious disease. Google it." The window washing seemed to suddenly call him away and off he went. If I knew I was going to be incinerated later this year I certainly wouldn't be consuming anything resembling quinoa. I would be stocking my freezer with Cherry Garcia and German Chocolate ice cream and live heartily on that, perhaps sullying my wool to the point where it wouldn't pass the good sheep detector. Somehow being the good sheep is filled with pratfalls and organic grains, a treacherous and unhappy path to the halls of righteousness. I'll stick with rest of the weak-willed flock. I'll join the swaying resigned backs of ruminants being led away to the caves of doom.

The Kicking Circle

John Castell

Sixth grade stole the comfortable, hand-me-down traditions of Pines Lake elementary and dragged me through the doors to three nasty years of ridicule and alienation at Schuyler Colfax Middle School. I would no longer hop from rock to rock on the three-minute walk from home to school. Now I crammed into a yellow bus that arrived on the corner at 7:00 a.m. sharp. Swarms of neighborhood kids emerged from houses with lopsided bed hair and nappy pullovers woven with stale kitchen odors from last night's dinner.

Some days I looked, in wistful thought, at the elementary school just beyond the bus stop and remembered the licorice black hair and ruby red lipstick of the perfect Miss Solara, my first grade teacher. She would remain behind as perennial mother to welcome each year's new clutch of tiny pupils with open, milk white arms. I savored those memories of holiday construction paper decorations, Halloween costume pageants and school plays that filled me with warm nostalgia and simplicity. Age 12 came without alliances or securities and made clear a truth; my naïve childhood self-esteem had vanished.

One morning, dad stood me in front of him at his worn armchair and eyed me over; that my hair was combed, shirt and pants were clean and shoes polished. Outside the bay window I saw a gray winter morning of leafless trees and dirty snow banks left by plows during the night. I curled a bag lunch between anxious, nail-bitten fingers. A whiff of tuna sandwich and red delicious apple escaped as I gripped tighter anticipating the start of another school day. When dad completed his inspection, I leaned towards him to kiss him goodbye as I had always done. Today he stopped me and held me back at the shoulders.

"No!" he said. "You're a big boy now. You go to a big school where boys don't kiss their fathers."

His large voice and hands pushed me an arm's length away and I understood I was not to kiss him again. He didn't want to know *me* but for me to act more like other boys. His protective wing lifted and was gone. My heart objected but resigned in silence like leaves in the fall.

I gathered my books and science fair project and made a run for the bus that just pulled up with its red lights bouncing back and forth. I found an empty seat and stared through the grimy window back at my house, hidden between the oak trees. The bus leaned with the weight of each kid that climbed aboard, until the driver pulled the door handle shut and lurched forward to the next stop.

When we arrived at school, the boys pushed out of the bus into a huddle away from the line-up to go inside for homeroom. The winter ground was slippery and coated in a thick layer of black ice. I noticed a single red maple leaf that lay trapped underneath. I tried to fit in with the boys; mimicked their budding masculinity and laughed along as we played. A voice inside urged me to try and fit in; become part of the flock. Don't be different. *Maybe someone will like me.*

One boy found a frozen blackbird on the ground below a classroom window.

"Hey, lookit this guys!"

With hands still in his pockets for warmth, he used the side of his foot to skid it over for us to see.

We circled around to look, and the others made a game of booting it back and forth between them at their center. I stood back and felt sympathy for the bird; wishing them to stop. The feathers were a dark, shiny, blue-black and the eyes fixed open. They stared inside me to a blackness, a void; the space my twin brother's drowning accident left when we were five.

"How would you like it, if it were you frozen dead and someone kicked you around like that?"

I heard the words exit my mouth and change the atmosphere. Would I regret having said my feelings out loud?

"Why do you care?" replied the toughest boy.

I smelled the cigarettes and Bazooka bubble gum in his words. I backed away.

Spotting the science fair project under my arm he added, "And what's that you're holding, a goddamned flower? Look at this guys, he's got a pretty flower for the teacher! Ha-ha! I'm gonna call you 'Petunia.'"

The boys in his circle followed the leader and laughed while others shied away and whispered in uneasy quiet. Popular girls stood nearby and noticed the rowdy outburst. They smiled with silver braces into notebooks perched in their arms. Other boys in the huddle moved away from me and returned to the bird-on-ice game until the homeroom bell rang.

We lined up and entered the school single file, then ran to our lockers. I unlocked the door and revealed my cascade of recently applied groovy flower and smiley stickers in sunny yellow and pink. I dumped some unneeded books and grabbed my science project to rush to the first class.

Mrs. Graye walked around the room and observed us as we worked on science fair projects. My display presented a flower's growth cycle. I began with a piece of wood I found in the basement, that used to be the front of my baby crib.

The board showcased the stages of germination from seed to blossom. I painted illustrations and made a large tissue paper flower with a flashy gold foil sun attached. The flower moved back and forth to show how it followed sunlight. Plastic tubes represented roots with dyed green water that bubbled through them with the help of a fish tank pump.

The teacher didn't ask me much about it. I wasn't the blue ribbon scholar she had hoped to cultivate. This creation was more artistic than scientific.

After Biology we had five minutes to get to our lockers and to the next class. A group of girls approached. One asked if I would make a flower for her like the one on my project. I didn't notice that the other five girls had surrounded me. I recognized them from class. In seconds, they began to kick at my shins and ankles and calves. No teacher was around to notice. I dropped my unwieldy project and my books fell on top; crushing the delicate blossom. I tried to push away from them but they had captured me and I froze in their trap. The kicks continued. My eyes welled from the pain. If I called out, the boys wouldn't help me. I saw no escape. The final bell rang and the girls hurried away dropping the words "fag" and "queer" behind them. I didn't know what the words meant. I was in shock.

Lifting my pant legs exposed many cuts and scrapes draped in red blood. The pain throbbed. I hid them in shame so no one would notice. As I raised myself up, I saw that the halls had emptied. The sun had pierced through the gray day and laid brilliant streams of golden light across the floor. *Don't kiss your father. Don't tell. Be yourself. Listen to your natural instincts.* Thoughts collided in my head. I learned that I am allowed to be here. I had survived and would grow wherever I was planted.

Black Fire

Martha Kinkade

If today was the birth
Of my world, then the skin
Between my legs would moisten,
Dried blooms would scatter
And wind would carry
Until dust became eternity.

These flames grab higher,
Scorch my heal
Peeling layers of skin
Into whispering tendrils.

Bones crack, shatter with smoke.
Behold the beauty of bold black
    The Mother of All.

More

Sylvia Levinson

My television tells me to
supersize it. Internet pop-ups

offer two for the price of one.
The child actress, all ringlets

and gap-toothed, in the smartphone
ad, is absolutely sure "more is better."

What difference in a plethora?
Is there greater worth in multitudes?
A swarm of bees, a field of poppies?

Here on Maui, outside the window,
a needle-sharp downpour,

baptizes the hot afternoon,
the plants, the sky.

A honeycreeper, shakes out
her feathers, inserts her long beak

down a firecracker bloom, lipstick-red.
On the rock wall, a lime green gecko

rests, his neon throat pulsing.
Toward the ocean, a rainbow.

Picture Day

Anita Knowles

Sylvia knew the importance of Picture Day, even as a freshman. Over the years she had spent hours with her great aunt, Nana B, flipping through the pages of her four black and white yearbooks from Conjunction High School, 1959-1962, scanning the photographs of girls with flips curls and bouffant hair-do's that required enough Aqua Net to blow a hole the size of Cleveland in the ozone layer.

Sylvia had witnessed the timeless reach of a high school picture, seen firsthand how that single, contrived pose forever defined an entire year of a girl's life. The eight thousand pictures Sylvia captured on her Samsung and shared on Snapchat fell to the jaws of history within seconds, mere morsels of fodder for the hungry beast she and her generation depended on for relating to one another.

But a high school photograph? Immortal.

Four photos, four years. Four awkward profiles, necks bent in uncomfortable angles, cemented in history as freshman, sophomore, junior and the penultimate pose, the senior portrait, all mile markers of a teenager's journey through the treacherous switchbacks of puberty.

Four photographs that ride a woman's back through graduation; college; the abandonment of virginity; dropping out of college; marriage; children; the attempt at re-entering the work force after maternity leave; inevitable divorce; custody and child support battles; a stint in rehab; the second marriage; step children who would just as soon stab you in your sleep; two mid-life crises; the renunciation of marriage as an institution;

reading glasses; perimenopause; brief affairs with imago therapy, sweat lodges and a smoking hot Republican from Pittsburgh; hemorrhoids; dreams of being a grandma; the heart-breaking news that your son is gay, your daughter found her passion on a secluded farm in Idaho, and your only grandchild is a toothless Mastiff named Ron Jeremy; the discovery of medical brownies to help with the arthritis; the real menopause; incidental pants peeing in the face of unexpected jokes; reunions at ten, twenty-five, forty and fifty years; and in Nana B's case, stomach cancer that killed her ninety-nine days from diagnosis despite "aggressive" chemo, homeopathic remedies shipped from Nepal and what everyone called an "extraordinary fighting spirit."

Four photographs that, along with ninety-six others, flashed across a flat screen TV for the duration of Nana B's calling hours at Pickerington's Funeral Home on Apple Avenue. A well-intentioned but feeble attempt at confirming what everyone proclaimed as they passed by her urn and whispered, "She lived a good life."

Father's Day
June 15, 2014

Nancy Dimsdale

His mind peeled away
Like the cracked shell
Of a hard-boiled egg
Sometimes making a clean break
Sometimes sticky and reluctant.

Fading Voices

David Raines

Sun paints a canvas sky
ablaze in amber fire
Wind breathes softly through an
empty necropolis
sweeping the smoky scent
of used up kindling
on a cold, cold, so cold
February evening
Feral felines emerge
as evening douses day
Fading voices softly
bid me please come away
My vision swims as I
pretend I do not hear

Commandments

Rebecca Romani

Theoretically,
My neighbor is here
To teach me
Humility,
Compassion,
Patience,
Tolerance…
(all good things,
in theory…)
I have learned
How to call
911,
How to say:
Child Welfare Check,
Nuisance,
Assault…
How to give
My address
Succinctly,
To talk to cops,
To listen for blows,
To know the difference
Between
An earthquake
And my neighbor
Stomping around so hard
It shakes my windows.

Perhaps,
Love Thy Neighbor
Includes
An intervention.

Bukowski, I Dreamed

Mike Hedrick

I dreamed…

I woke with Bukowski
gargling
in the bathroom
down a flop-house hall
the rough timbre of his ravaged
throat
like the last notes of jazz
heard on 6th Street at 2:00 a.m.
I never played the ponies
much
nor closed a bar
and women they cost
money.
he shuffles past my
door
a cough like gravel rolling off a tin roof.
he types all the time in his room
alone
the clatter of keys
like the mutter of drunks in bars
across L.A.
he types like the rains won't ever
stop
and we need more.

Family Secrets

Diane Malloy

Atlanta: 1965

It was not a dry heat, and the ladies were wilting like week-old roses. They revived when Connor strode in beaming, resplendent in a still-crisp linen suit.

"Mother..." He bent to kiss her cheek. "Aunt Camille," his lips pressed her hand. He peppered the parlor with compliments, "Ladies, you're looking more lovely each time I see you." They tittered and squirmed in response. "Excuse the intrusion, Mother, but I have news!"

His mother paused her teapot mid-pour and angled a brow.

"I...was just asked to run for Congress!" Disbelief and delight played across his features.

The ladies erupted in good wishes and support but his mother's smile was restrained. She knew what this would mean: inquiries; every closet searched for skeletons. Her secret would have to stay buried where scandal seekers would never find it.

"Well, congratulations, dear. Have you agreed to run?"

"I told them I was honored and that, of course, I'd consider it, seriously." He paced the Oriental rug. "And, they could expect my answer on Monday."

Camille spoke up, "Of course you must, dear, to further Uncle Reggie's legacy..." She pressed a palm to her chest; her bosom expanded. "He'd be so proud, bless his soul." They went silent a moment honoring Reggie's passing a decade earlier.

Sally Ann dimpled and fluttered, "We'd all be proud: our Connor, a Congressman!" She sniffed quietly.

No nonsense Lillian took over, "Darling, you have our backing. And we'll tell everyone we know, that they absolutely *must* vote for you." Her plan in motion, she nodded with finality.

Connor smiled and decided to humor these dear ladies who'd practically raised him. He thumbed his lapels, propped one foot on the blue brocade ottoman. "My esteemed constituents, I am humbled and will do my utmost to serve with integrity." He turned, "Mother? What say you?"

She considered. "If that's what you wish, dear. I only want your happiness." Then her eyes glanced heavenward. "The job has great benefits. You could do such good. But, it also requires great sacrifice."

She made a mental note to visit Albert the next day. With his CIA prowess, he could bury a secret when necessary.

Connor nodded. "That's true, *and* the reason I held off deciding." His slow exhale bespoke his uncertainty. "Well, ladies, seems I have some pondering to do, so I'll let you get back to your tea."

With hugs and kisses all around, he strode back out, a bounce in his stride.

Later Connor's mother took to her room. She opened the closet and pulled a locked box from the top shelf. Inside was a birth certificate. Would it still pass, she wondered.

~~~~~~~~~~~~~~~~~~~~~~~~~~~~~~~~~~~~~

Dublin: 1930

The parents of the conjoined infants knew the procedure was risky but the prognosis, favorable. With trusting hearts they had consented to the surgery and now the twins were separated and sutured, identical with only opposite scars marking any difference.

As a nurse was prepping the babies for the recovery room, she noticed that one had stopped breathing. "Doctor!" The surgeon came over and shook his head. The tiny body was too fragile for more interventions, so he let nature and God have their way. Placing his hand over the tiny face he said a quick prayer and went to tell the parents.

Hearing the news, the mother's voice broke, "I can't." She buried her face in her husband's shoulder.

"I know…sweetheart." He held her against him and held back his own tears. His voice was husky when he spoke. "Well… at least we have one healthy boy to take back home." His wife's sobs rocked him.

Overwhelmed, the husband instructed the surgeon to have the morbid infant taken away. "And Doctor…have your priest bless it first?" he asked. Then he was done.

Both infants were wrapped in blankets. One was taken to recovery by a nurse, the other to the morgue by a young orderly. The parents grieved the loss of the one, but reminded themselves the surgery had been necessary; they had done the right thing. They would take their healthy baby home soon, and put guilt and grief behind them. That was all they could do.

As the young orderly neared the morgue with the covered body, he felt a slight movement in his hands. He stopped and looked down; saw nothing and thought he'd imagined it. He continued on then heard a faint sound. He'd heard of air escaping from a corpse minutes after the demise and assumed this was the case. "Poor little lad," he thought.

His assumption proved wrong once he got inside the morgue and the blanket started moving forcefully. A muted squeak swelled to a wail.

He held his breath and pulled back the blanket. The tiny body was moving indeed. Its eyes squeezed shut and its fisted arms flailed in fury. Liam's eyes swept the morgue and saw only Margaret Gallagher mopping the floor. He fought to control the squirming infant and looked at her helplessly.

Margaret's mouth flew open. "What are you doing with that in here?"

"It was dead. They told me it was dead. I saw for myself." Liam blessed himself. "God, Margaret, is it a miracle?"

"By the sainted Mother, likely a miracle, lad." Her mouth twitched. "What are you going to do?"

He looked at her, then remembered his darling Katie at

home, heartbroken after her third miscarriage in as many years. His brain wheeled.

"Oh...I'll take him back then, won't I?"

"Yes, of course, you will. Good lad." Margaret turned back to her mopping.

The orderly covered the infant again and walked out. He quickened his pace down the hall towards the nurse's station, but made a quick turn towards a stairwell.

"Hey Boyo, ready to pop out for some lunch?" his mate, Brian, yelled from down the hall.

"Can't today. Sorry. Have an errand for the Missus."

"Maybe tomorrow, then?" Brian waved him off.

No one seemed concerned about an orderly taking his lunch break when Liam turned his back and hurried through the stairwell door. At the bottom of the stairs, he shoved through the exit door and walked casually to his car. He held his bundle tightly under an arm then checked it again inside the car. The baby had gone silent, but his eyes were open and he was still breathing.

"Hang on, there, laddie." He felt the first twinge of affection for the tiny fighter. "Guess what! You're going home."

He didn't analyze his decision, just kept his foot on the gas pedal and was home in 15 minutes. Katie was just sitting down to her meal.

"Liam! What a nice surprise. You're here to join me for lunch, then?"

He hesitated and presented his parcel.

"What have you got there?" Her eyes twinkled. "You've brought me a present?"

His shoulders lifted; his smile, half grimace. "I guess I have after a fashion." He unwrapped the blanket revealing the infant.

Katie's hand flew to her mouth. "Oh, dear God! Liam, what in the Lord's name have you done?"

~~~~~~~~~~~~~~~~~~~~~~~~~~~~~~~~~~~~~

After the infant was fed, cleaned, and put down between soft pillows, Liam and Katie faced each other on the faded couch. Shock and disbelief, wonder and horror swept their faces. Katie finally rubbed her temple. "What are we doing, Liam? This can't be right!"

"Katie, my love, they left him for dead. Besides they have another and we have none. Where's the harm?"

"Liam! It's *their* baby. They have a right to know!"

Head bowed, he seemed to wrestle an inner conflict. Then he leaned towards her. His voice was firm. "I look at it like this: it was given to me and I think God brought it back so *we* could raise it. It's a gift."

While he spoke, Katie fingered her rosary beads, praying for guidance. Maybe he was right and it was true. From what he had said, the baby had died, and the parents didn't want it. It took her only a second to decide that her prayers had been answered. *Yes.* Yes, she wanted it. Wanted him.

"Yes, Liam. I think you may be right. So should we? Keep him?" The whisper belied her swirling terror and elation.

"Do you want to? Can we do it?"

Katie's heart was already swelling. "Yes, we can! But, he needs proper care. Medicine. And what do we tell people? What about where he came from?" They sat silently a moment. Then Katie's hand flew to her mouth. "Oh Lord, the hospital? Surely they'll find he's gone missing?" In his haste Liam hadn't thought that far ahead. "If we keep him, Katie, I don't think we can stay here! I think we have to leave Dublin, maybe Ireland. It's too late to go back now. Everything's changed."

Katie looked around the humble but tidy apartment they'd called home since their wedding. She thought of their families. Could they just leave everyone, everything? Could anyone ever know the truth? "We have to leave now, don't we?"

'Fraid so, love. What about America? Maybe the South? Make a new life…"

Katie could hardly breathe. Her head spun from the enormity of what they were facing. Then the infant's cry brought reality into sharp focus and both jumped up to respond. They rushed in and Katie picked up the baby. "Hush, little one." She looked at Liam. "He'll need a name."

"That he will."

"I've always liked Connor. It was my grandfather's name."

"I like it, too." He patted the baby's head. "So, Connor, are you ready to become an American?" The baby looked at him and he seemed to smile.

On Your 72nd Birthday

Dania Brett

Icebox bright fluorescent light
Blasts its sheen in black and white
With need and dread to bind me here I find you
Around each corner in the glass
Your flesh displayed upon the wrack
The red flags of your ecstasy proclaiming

Minor players in the game
Referees of hope and shame
Tasted truth yet hurried past the crime scene
Kaleidoscopic silent screams
Drifted down with autumn leaves
And all bore witness to the changing season

Your trench coat in the corn midwest
The playground porn you wielded best
Are filed away from view but not forgotten
Handmade suits of polished cloth
Courtroom wit and princely charm
Your tissue paper gauze now soiled and rotting

The sex you cradle barely there
You grip the railing of your chair
And reach for glory days not worth recalling
I burn with rage you fade with name
I may be nothing but your blame
Yet there you sit and here I am still standing

The Mikado

Jill G. Hall

I see our photo
in the scrapbook
and think of that summer
when we were twenty-five.

You running late into
the dressing room
with a loveliness
sublime to warm up
our soprano voices,
tuck blonde curls
into geisha wigs,
paint faces white,
drape satin kimonos
over lacy undergarments
and tie obis on slim waists.

We wait in the wings
and flirt with boys
from the cast until
the orchestra calls.
Sashi-ashi style shuffling
onstage, your voice lifts like
a rainbow to the crowd.

Our fans flick open
on cue. Beside me

you shine radiant
as the sun. I am
a coolie basking
in your glory.

Where are you now?

I silently pray, Broadway.
But last I'd heard
you'd moved to Seattle,
married and had a child.

Kissing Rosalie

Steve Bruno

I was a junior in high school. I was a smart kid, excelling in almost every academic endeavor. I was not an athlete. I didn't know much about life in general. But one thing I knew was an absolute certainty: I wanted to kiss Rosalie Foster.

Rosalie wasn't the best-looking girl in our class. She wouldn't win any Homecoming Queen or Prom Queen contests. But she was definitely pretty in a conservative egghead sort of way. Like me she was smart. She was popular. She had a good personality and was nice to everyone. We had sat next to each other in Latin class for the past two years. Miss Avril, who definitely must have personally known Julius Caesar, demanded that pupils in her Latin class sit in alphabetical order. I, Joe Franklin, sat next to Rosalie Foster who sat next to Erica Edwards who sat next to Matt Eason. Matt, Erica, Rosalie and I were the brains of the Latin class. So we became the Four Amici. There was a Latin Club that you had to join if you wanted to get an "A" in the class. The four of us took turns rotating through the offices of president, secretary, treasurer, and chairman of the Saturnalia, the annual shindig for Latin students. It isn't that any of us loved the language of Latin or the culture of ancient Rome. It's just that we all wanted to get into good colleges and knew that getting an "A" in Latin might help. Anyway, I loved going to Latin class, knowing that I would be sitting next to my dream girl, Rosalie. I was always very nice to her and she was nice to me. She wasn't nice enough to me to give me any hope of ever kissing her. But I wasn't going to give up. I couldn't give up if I had wanted to. It had become more than an obsession. It had become a self-imposed litmus test to establish my manhood.

Rosalie dressed nicely, but didn't use too much makeup, like some of the girls. She used just a touch of eyeliner and face blush. You wouldn't notice it unless, like me, you were studying every pore on her body that was exposed. But her lips! She almost always wore pinkish lipstick that was covered with a shiny white gloss. It gave her mouth a frosted look. It was definitely kissable. It was definitely very kissable. I often wondered if she did that so someone would kiss her. Not every someone, of course, but some someones. The question was: was I one of the someones? I doubted it. It weighed on me.

Rosalie was almost perfect in every way. She was perfect for me because, in many ways, we were alter egos. We shared many interests, we carried ourselves the same way—always being friendly to everyone, regardless of social rank, and we were both smart and wanted to go to a good college. We shared friends, primarily Erica and Matt. We even went to the same church. I tried to figure out which Mass her family always went to so I could ask my dad if we could attend that Mass. The trouble was, her family didn't seem to choose the same time from one Sunday to the next. So I would only occasionally see her in church. It really was my only reason for going to church.

Unfortunately, Rosalie's one flaw was a big one. It was one that made ever kissing her practically impossible. It was her father. He was Mr. Foster, vice-principal of the school. He was also Coach Foster, the football coach. Now I don't want to say that Mr. Foster was a tyrant. But, I think to properly describe the environment I was working in—the obstacle I had to overcome, I should really say he was a tyrant. In his role as vice-principal, he was the advisor to the student council. I was a prominent member of the student council. Unfortunately for both of us I didn't take what he said at face value. I challenged authority. For example, when we were discussing the budget (how we were going to allocate the funds that had been raised by selling memberships in the student body to the students) I thought the cheerleaders were scheduled to receive a disproportionate amount of money, especially in comparison to clubs like the chess club or the Honor

Society (of which I was president). When I stated my opinion, Mr. Foster's face turned bright red. He said, "Those cheerleaders work at every athletic game we play, representing the entire student body. Their uniforms have to be attractive and clean. They deserve the best we can afford."

I pointed out that there were only eight cheerleaders and there were twenty-four members of the chess club and eight-four members of the Honor Society. And that the chess club competed against other schools to uphold the reputation of Madison High and the Honor Society could benefit from a couple computers to complete college applications. These arguments only managed to make Mr. Foster's face redder. When I said, "Maybe it's time to vote on it," Mr. Foster raised his hand and said, "There just isn't enough money to go around to everyone. The cheerleaders have already bought their uniforms and we can't get the money back."

I said, "So this budget is a foregone conclusion. There's really no point in discussing it or voting on it, even though it's the students' money and not the school's."

He was at a loss for words, and that wasn't good for me. He knew I had outwitted him and he didn't accept someone showing him up without holding a lifelong grudge. Did I really think I was ever going to get to kiss Rosalie?

What was even worse was the fact that, to Coach Foster, you weren't anything if you weren't a football player. I could have won the Nobel Prize and been elected to the United States Senate (I know, unlikely as a high-school junior, right?), but if I wasn't on the football team, I was nobody. Matt was on the football team and he seemed to be buddies with Coach Foster, like all the football players were. Matt told me his coaching style was similar to that of General George Patton. But the players wanted to earn a football letter so they could wear those stupid lettermen's jackets to school, to church, to the movies, to the dentist—literally to everywhere. It isn't as if this Patton-like approach to coaching was working. Madison had been four-and-six the last two years. But it seemed Coach Foster was ingrained as the coach for all perpetuity.

So for all these reasons whenever Mr. Foster had to look

at me he looked at me as a bull might look at a fly who had dared to perch on his tail. He knew he could flick me off anytime he chose, but I was never worth the effort.

But back to Rosalie. Yet another reason why I probably was never going to kiss her was the fact that she had a boyfriend. I called him "Doug the Hunk." He was brawny, somewhat intelligent and, most of all, he was a football player. You could see Coach Foster beam whenever Doug came into view. Rosalie seemed to beam, too. Doug wasn't a bad guy. He just wasn't me. I was smarter, had more of a future and loved Rosalie more passionately than Doug ever could. How did I know this? Because I loved her more than anyone ever could love another. Or so I was convinced. I really wasn't so sure about that. But I was definitely sure than I wanted to kiss her more than anyone had ever wanted to kiss another person. Those lips! I couldn't get them out of my head. I would go to sleep thinking of how they would feel, how they would taste, how they would say the words I longed to hear: "Kiss me."

Doug and Rosalie had been going together for about six months. It was nearing Prom time and I hadn't planned on going. The previous year Matt had taken Rosalie. But this year Matt was going to take Erica. That left good old Joe Amicus out in the cold. I tried not to think about it. I imagined the Four Amici less Joe plus Doug would be double dating. I mentioned it to Matt about two weeks before the dance. "Oh, no," he said. "Rosalie and Doug broke up about ten days ago. Erica said Rosalie is planning on staying home. Maybe you should ask her."

WHAT?! WHAT?! Could I believe my ears? It wasn't possible, was it? I could never be this lucky. Well, it wasn't a done deal yet. I still had Mr. Foster, the Obstacle, to overcome. And who knew if Rosalie could stand the sight of me? She had acted like she could. But I was no expert in the vagaries of women's minds or hearts.

I decided to think about it for a day—not to rush into things and blurt out a question to Rosalie, like some dumb lovestruck fool, even though I definitely was a dumb lovestruck fool. That night I thought about how I was going to ask her. It was true that this all was probably futile since if she told her father she was going to the Prom with me he probably would have killed her or, at least, kicked her out of the house. But I wasn't going to let him ruin my life any more than he already had. If she turned me down I wouldn't ask the reason. I would know her father was the reason. It would be better than finding out she didn't like me.

The next day, in Latin class, I asked her if I could have a word with her after class. She said, "Sure." When the room had emptied after the bell had rung, with my heart in my throat and on my sleeve I said to Rosalie, "I know you probably have already made arrangements. But if you haven't I was wondering if you might like to go to the Prom with me." There. I had done it. Hooray for me. I wasn't the wimp that Mr. Foster thought I was, was I?

"Sure, thanks," was Rosalie's unexpected reply.

"See you later," I stammered out.

"Sure, thanks"? That's what she had said? I was dumbfounded. It was as if she had been expecting me to ask her to the Prom. Or as if some hand in the cosmos was manipulating strings and making her mouth say words I wanted to hear, without giving her the option of making the decision on her own. Whatever the reason, I was ecstatic. I couldn't control my smile. I couldn't wait to ask Matt if we could double date with him and Erica. Actually, I just wanted him to know that Rosalie was going with me. I wanted his admiration that I had achieved this fete. I got it. He was pleased for me and for all of us. Going together would make it much more fun and not so scary. At that age being alone with a person of the opposite sex could be frightening, especially if you really cared for them.

To my dismay, I started to think about all this. Rosalie hadn't yet told (or asked) her father. What if Mr. Pig-headed Jock told her she couldn't go with me? That was entirely possible. Would she defy him, or cave to his disapproval? I didn't know. The next twenty-four hours were crucial, I decided. I went home and sat by the phone, waiting for all hell to break loose.

Luckily for me, the same hand from the cosmos that had made Rosalie say "yes" to me kept things intact throughout the night and the entire next day at school. I was becoming more and more confident in the entire situation when another thought entered my fractured and terrified mind. What if things went well? We had a wonderful time and then I took her home and then…the kiss. The Kiss. I was going to get to kiss Rosalie. Finally. At least I hoped I would get to kiss her. What if things didn't go well? Or what if they did and she just didn't want to kiss me? What if she was using me to get Doug back? What if her father was waiting at the door for us? What if she let me kiss her and I was a horrible kisser? What if, what if, what if? It never stopped.

Until the day of the Prom, I tried to stay out of Doug the Hunk's eyesight. I didn't want a confrontation in front of the entire student body. I was sure it would be a confrontation I would lose, not only because Doug was so much stronger and physical than I was, but because he and Rosalie had a history I didn't have with her. Time was on his side. I was an interloper, a passing fancy, a tool Rosalie could use to apply leverage to her position with Doug. Was that what was happening here? This seemed to be my one shot to plant my flag into Rosalie's heart. I hoped I wouldn't blow it.

Finally the day of the Prom arrived. The four of us were going to meet at the Braveheart Restaurant (good name, huh?), have a great dinner, then go to the dance. Of course I was nervous. But I talked myself into thinking I had nothing to lose. Who was I kidding? I had everything to lose. If I blew it in any way I probably wouldn't get to kiss Rosalie. I wasn't sure I could live with myself if that happened.

When I went to the door to pick her up, Mr. Foster was nowhere in sight. I was so thankful. Mrs. Foster answered the door. She was such a nice lady. Why she had ever saddled herself with such a palooka was beyond me. Anyway, Mrs. Foster, smiling, asked me to come in and wait for Rosalie by sitting on the couch in the living room. I did. Mrs. Foster made small talk with me while my heart tried to gear down to about two-hundred beats per minute. Soon Mrs. Foster turned her eyes to the stairwell from the second floor. I did the same and I saw Rosalie as I had never seen her. She was gorgeous! She was wearing a lavender dress with purple highlights. Her hair had a lavender net of some sort in it and I saw that the purple orchid corsage I had brought her would look perfect on her bodice. Her face looked glittery and her mouth—the focus of my attention for so many years—was purpley-red and frosted, as usual. As I stood up I almost fell down.

"Hi," said the goddess.

"Hi," replied the nimrod.

With that I pinned the corsage on her and off we went.

Everything went fine at the restaurant. Erica looked lovely, Matt looked lovely, everyone looked lovely. All four of us had lobster and filet mignon. Why not? This was a once-in-a-lifetime meal. If I died tomorrow (which wasn't out of the question, it seemed) I would have had a great last meal and I would have kissed Rosalie (I hoped). I would be ready to die, I told myself.

The Prom itself was more fun than I had imagined. Rosalie seemed to be relaxed, which made me feel more relaxed. We danced; I had my arms around her at last. She didn't seem to pull away or resist—a good sign, I thought. When the music became slow and romantic, our cheeks touched as our faces turned away from each other. I even took an opportunity to brush her cheek with my lips. I'm sure she didn't notice. I told myself I was finally kissing Rosalie, but I knew I was fooling myself. We had our pictures taken, like all Prom couples do. We traded partners with Matt and Erica for a couple of dances. I tried to concentrate on Erica and her banter, but it was asking too much of the dumb lovestruck fool.

As the evening was winding down, the music seemed to get generally slower and more romantic. Rosalie melted more easily into my arms. We held each other closer. There was no doubt in my mind that there would be at least one good kiss at the end of the night. Could this be the start of my dream life? I wouldn't let myself think so. Things this great just don't happen to people like me. I don't know why, they just don't. But I was enjoying the moment more than I ever had thought possible. This was how life was meant to be lived—with the girl of your dreams in your arms.

The dance ended. Rosalie and I got into my car and I started to drive her home. She said, "I had a really nice time tonight, Joe." As sweet as that sounds it really set off alarm bells in my mind. Was she making her final farewell, wrapping up the night so, when I stopped in front of her house she could open her car door and run out by herself? Would she sprint to her house's door and let herself in without giving me a ghost of a chance to kiss her? I tried to extend the conversation.

"I've always imagined a night like this: the two of us being together and dancing. It was better than I had ever imagined it would be," I admitted.

Rosalie smiled a genuine smile and said, "I'm glad. We've always gotten along well with each other, haven't we?"

I replied, "Yes, and I think I know the reason for that. I think we're very much alike. Our temperaments are alike and we have a lot of things in common. It's nice." I hoped this might warm things up a bit between us, but feared it wouldn't be enough to prevent Rosalie from bolting for her front door. I would soon find out.

I pulled up in front of her house and turned off the motor. Rosalie didn't move. That was a good sign. So I hopped out of the car and walked around to her side of the car. I opened the door for her and she slowly got out and held my hand while we walked to her doorstep. There was a porch light over the stoop which over-illuminated the area, as far as I was concerned. But one side of the cement porch was darker than the other. I pulled her to the darker side. She came willingly. I put my hand behind her head, cocked my face at about a thirty-degree angle and pulled her lips to mine. I kissed her. And she kissed me. It was a perfect kiss. By perfect I mean it had just the right amount of pressure, just the right amount of moisture and was the perfect duration—about six seconds. I pulled back from her and looked at her face. She smiled warmly at me. As I had been hoping for so long, it was the Kiss of the Century. So I went in again. This time there was more pressure, more moisture and more duration. And there was some tongue. Not a lot, but some. The kiss lasted about fifteen seconds. I pulled away from her and looked straight into her beautiful eyes. I was hoping to see love. But I knew I wouldn't. What I did see was affection and kindness. Then I hugged her. I held her for about thirty seconds and then she pulled away from me ever-so-slowly, smiled at me for one last time and said, "Goodnight, Joe".

I said, "Goodnight, Rosalie." What else could I have said? "I love you, Rosalie. But, of course you knew that." Or how about, "My dreams came true when I kissed you." No. No. I wasn't a song lyricist and I wasn't going to hit the poor girl over the head with my passion. She had been wonderful to me. She was a great human being. I didn't want to pressure her or saddle her with my crazy desire for her. She had enough to deal with. If we had a future it would happen. If we didn't, I wanted this moment to be perfect, both for Rosalie and for me. It was. I had kissed Rosalie. And she had kissed me. I had visited heaven. I could face whatever the future brought satisfied and unafraid.

Going Home

Sumilu Cue

In her tidy room, big enough for a dresser, a twin bed, a nightstand, and a chair, she packed a small bag. She did not have much. She never had and it never bothered her. Outside an onshore breeze pushed a cold grey fog inland. The heavy mist enveloped the small homes on the hillside, which faced west towards Mission Bay, but she did not see it. In her mind she saw bright, hazy, hot, humid streets where drivers and passengers zoomed around on two wheeled mopeds and motorcycles past slower, larger automobiles and jeeps, past two, three, four, and five story buildings that were flushed against their neighbors. In her tidy room, Doanh Thi Tran hummed a discordant melody in a thin falsetto.

There was a soft knock on the door before a woman opened the door and poked her head into the room. "Má, why are you packing?"

"We go Da Nang. Em Chinh, why no ready? We go Da Nang."

The woman winced, then smiled. "I'm not Em Chinh. I'm Terrie, your daughter, Má, remember?"

Doahn looked up at Terrie and grabbed her arm, pulling down and holding tight. "Em, you no see Má? Cha? Why you no ready?" The wrinkled skin around her eyes furrowed with worry. "We go now, we go now. No miss train."

"Yes, train. Má, you're not in Saigon." Terrie pried her mother's fingers off her arm and shook out her numb hand. "Come. I have your breakfast ready for you."

~~~~~~~~~~~~~~~~~~~~~~~~~~~~~~~~~

A jingle of keys and then there was muffled swearing from the other side of the front door. "Wait, I'll be right there," yelled Terrie as she settled her mother into a chair at the round kitchen table. There were two bangs on the door. Terrie could feel the frustration behind them and she shook her head.

Tired, she thought, as she walked to the door. It was only a few steps from the kitchen, but it seemed so far away. There were a few more impatient raps and she sighed. She peeked out the window next to the door and saw her son. She reached into her pocket, pulled out a small set of keys and unlocked the deadbolt keeping him on the other side.

"Mom, what the hey?" he asked when she stepped aside to let him in.

"I have a key for you. You don't check your messages? Má took a walk. The police found her on Fiesta Island. I changed the lock, so she doesn't let herself out."

"You have to keep a closer eye on her."

Why do children think they know better than their parents? Terrie thought. A retort formed on her lips, but she changed her mind and held it in. "Why are you here? Why are you not in school?"

"Presidents Day weekend, Mom. I have Monday off."

"It's Friday."

"I don't have any classes today."

Terrie felt the heat rise in her chest. Why do I work? Why do I pay tuition? she thought. She turned away and headed back to the kitchen and her mother.

~~~~~~~~~~~~~~~~~~~~~~~~~~~~~~~~~

Duk went into his bedroom and dropped his bags on the floor before heading into the kitchen. It was spare. His mother kept everything she could behind cabinets and in drawers. There was only a steaming pot of cháo ga or chicken rice porridge on the stove and small bowls of condiments on the kitchen table. He watched his mother reach into one of the cabinets. His stomach rumbled, but then he saw the lock on the refrigerator. That's new, he thought, before planting a kiss on the old woman's papery cheek.

"Hi, Bà ngoai! Happy to see me?" He sat down in a chair next to his grandmother.

His grandmother put her small hand on his. She leaned towards him and asked, "who?" before directing a torrent of Vietnamese at his mother.

Duk sat back. She's not with us anymore, he thought. There was no sadness, just recognition. He looked out at the sliding glass doors and saw a brightness in the thinning fog. He felt fingers touch his hair. His cheeks reddened, embarrassed that his short, spiky hair had caught his grandmother's attention and he saw his mother try to hide a smile.

"She wasn't this bad when I left at the beginning of the semester." He looked at his mother and wondered where the accusatory tone in his voice came from.

"Some days good, some days bad."

"That's it? That's all you have to say?"

"What's to say?" she said with a shrug of her shoulders.

He squirmed in his chair and it seemed, for the first time, he saw his mother growing old—the white strands in her dark hair, the lines around her mouth and eyes—weighed down by her familial responsibilities. He wondered, what would she say when he told her he was dropping out of school.

~~~~~~~~~~~~~~~~~~~~~~~~~~~~~~~~~~

She only felt confusion. The strange looking young man called her "bà ngoai" but she did not feel like a grandmother. How could she be "bà ngoai" to someone like him? Who are you? she thought over and over. Her younger sister and the young man spoke and she could not comprehend their conversation. *Speak Vietnamese!*

She pushed herself up from her chair and shuffled away, her hands reaching for the wall for balance.

"Má, eat!"

Packing, she had to finish packing. It was time to go home.

Ghost Tree

Seretta Martin

In this forest you stand like starched lace
a skeleton left from the fire
your thin trunk and fragile branches white
against the charred red bark of cedars
their slender voices, the wind's domain.
I will take care as I speak
breathing with the wounded
breathing with sunlight in your bare limbs
flickering like remembered flames
through what is left of the green canopy above us.
Puma tracks run through the dry creek bed
passing like quick blooms faint in shadows.

When I die stand my long white bones in this cedar grove
spread my fingers like twigs reaching
for light and the strength of wind.

Thea

Kenneth Zak

"We lost Thea on Tuesday," Cecil said. His stare was all glassy, looking at me, but through me too. The blue was drained from his eyes. I had just driven home from work, totally spent. Not ten steps from my front door. I put my hand onto his shoulder. All the workday bullshit ricocheting through my head stopped. It was the first time I had touched him since we shook hands seven months ago. Somehow it felt okay.

"I am so sorry," I said.

Cecil leaned heavily onto a cane. It looked like one of those fancy black jobs tapping the stage beneath a top hat in a cabaret. I had never before seen Cecil with a cane since we became neighbors. But I knew what a cane meant. My grandpa got around with a nicked walnut cane before we lost him. Gramps used to catch me with its crook and pull me over for a hug. I would loop it over the kitchen doorknob while we ate Sunday pot roast and fetch if for him when we were done. It made me special, the keeper of Excalibur.

The afternoon breeze could blow Cecil over except for that cane and my hand upon his shoulder. I didn't want to let go of him just yet. It felt like my Dad's shoulder. I can't remember Grandpa's shoulder so much anymore, but I know it was big and my hand small. Cecil had deflated about twenty-five pounds since Thea's stroke. That was two months ago. She never came home.

"We're having a memorial Sunday at five over at Christ Church," Cecil said.

"Thea was a spectacular woman. She was lucky to have you all these years," I said.

What bullshit. What did I know of *all those years*? We only met last February.

The white v-neck sagging around Cecil's chalky neck looked like the same t-shirt he sweated through those first few days after we had moved in. He puttered out front every day planting flowers, every movement a slow stutter. Mostly flats of red impatiens and marigolds, I think. White speckled pockets of alyssum spread around the borders too. Nice fragrance, that alyssum, always reminded me of walking up the broken sidewalk along my Grandparent's house back in Cleveland. Grandma was born, raised, married, had my dad and uncle and died all in the same house on Fleet Avenue. Talk about continuity. I heard so many family stories sitting on those back steps.

Maybe alyssum held the secret. I planted some once. It didn't take.

Straw hat, dirty white t-shirt, jean shorts and black socks and shoes. There was no pretense about my gardening neighbor. Cecil had built a little contraption that helped him get back up from his knees too. Sort of like a little balance beam with carpet rolled around it. Smart fella.

"I don't care about the blue ribbon," Cecil said to me that late February.

His cheeks were blotched red.

His middle-aged daughter was out there that day, kind of keeping an eye on old Cecil. I can't remember her name. She looked a little worried watching him work in the hot sun. She whispered to me once Cecil turned back to planting.

"Yes he does," she said.

"Blue ribbon?" I asked.

"The garden show judges come around on Saturday," she said.

Cecil was out there every day when I got home from work, tending to his flowerbed and going for another blue ribbon he didn't care about while Thea peeked out the living room window from her chair. It made our rented house next door feel more like a home, like a part of a little neighborhood with probably some good family stories from all those years. Thea didn't get out that much, even back then, what with her back and her legs and all that ailed her.

But one glorious afternoon I got to meet Thea. Boy was she something. A southern belle is a southern belle until the day…well, I hope forever. Thea dressed for every occasion, even just to sit outside to take some shade while Cecil planted violet pansies. For some reason, she got down from her porch to greet me. She emerged from the shadows in a blue blazer with a ruffled white collared blouse beneath. It was one of those ladies' blazers with an insignia patch sewn on the lapel. All I could make out was "Society of Southern" something or other before I was locked in her gaze.

Man, Thea was brilliant. I don't mean smart, well probably that too. But brilliant like a comet.

That first meeting all five-foot-nothing of Thea grinned up at me from her walker. My dad back home was already on an aluminum walker with little rubber wheels in the front. Dad wouldn't be making it back to anything as fancy as a cane. There's nothing romantic about a walker.

"Thea, short for Theodosia, named after the daughter of Aaron Burr," she said.

She dared lift one small hand from her walker. I took her hand. Well, actually I held the ends of her fingers. They were all veins and bones, blotched skin and gold and fingernails of scarlet perfection. She moved lightning fast to regain the grip on her walker.

"Ken," I said.

Shit, what else could I say? I wasn't named after anybody.

"What's your poison?" she asked.

"Wine, anything red," I said.

Thea bit her lip, like she was mulling whether to grant me a mulligan.

Cecil pushed up off his carpeted balance beam to get up from planting. Straight up he had probably been a formidable six three, but it didn't look like he got straight up anymore. His trunk was all twisted like one of those six oaks anchoring our front lawns. His skin was gnarled like the tree bark too.

"Well, my martinis are famous on Coronado," Cecil said.

"Then I'll need to try me one," I said.

"We'll invite you both for cocktails with a few couples you should meet," Thea said.

I liked how the word *cocktails* rolled from Thea's tongue, all perfectly aged southern polish, none of that trendy bullshit you hear in bars these days. It sure wasn't a Society of Southern Teetotalers patch on that blazer.

"Do you know the Simpsons?" she asked.

"I don't think so," I said.

I was pretty sure Thea wasn't talking about Homer and Marge.

"Pick a night that works best," Cecil said.

Well there I was, a long transplanted Yankee with a southern belle and a retired Vice Admiral rolling out the welcome wagon for Jamie and me.

"Tuesday's are best for me," Thea said.

"We'll need to book ahead, see if we can squeeze in between her bridge club and the Colonial Dames," Cecil said.

That cocktail party never happened.

But I still recall the bravado of Cecil that day after he used that contraption to mostly straighten up from planting, step off his lawn and onto the sidewalk in those black socks and shoes, and boast about his famous martinis with his precious Thea by his side. I even remember the very spot it all happened. Because it was where Cecil and I were standing when he told me she was gone.

"I'll be there on Sunday," I said.

Cecil looked at me and turned his head a bit, like a gray-snouted hound might. I wasn't sure if he was all there or not. Heck, I really never had been sure. He seemed to have his wits about him, but who knew. Still, he seemed to be waiting for something. So I told him.

"Oh, Jamie moved out last weekend."

I guess I felt I owed him that. Maybe I just needed to tell

somebody. But he was probably the only person I hadn't told. I hadn't seen Cecil much since Thea's stroke, and not since Jamie and me had been avoiding each other as amicably as we could. I guess old Cecil had been spending a lot of time at the nursing home, attending to the matter of his wife of sixty years dying. Moving trucks coming and going probably don't draw quite the same attention.

Or maybe Cecil already knew, because Jamie was the soil into which Cecil planted those flowers. She was the earth that anchored oaks. But I had become buried. Maybe both of us had.

"But what about your daughter?" Cecil asked.

"That was actually Jamie's daughter," I said.

He tilted his head again with that not-quite-reckoning look.

"I thought she was yours," he said and sighed.

Somehow all those past months I had kind of sensed that. Neighbors sort of get an impression of each other. A wave here, a hello hollered there. Maybe Cecil had seen me carry in Jaysa asleep from the car, her arms draped around my neck. A couple times she faked being asleep just so I'd carry her.

I knew he had seen me walking her home from elementary school couple times a week that spring, her little brown hand in my big freckly hand while we crossed the street. I remember she waved at him once from the back of my Vespa scooter that summer. Sometimes Jase hugged me around the stomach when we scooted around. Sometimes she was too cool to hug me. But even then, I could feel her little front leaning into my back. Cecil and Thea probably both saw Jase coming home with Jamie and me from fishing trips and birthday parties and soccer games and all those things we did for three seasons together.

But we really looked so different: Jase's caramel from her Portuguese father and Jamie's porcelain set against my sun-speckled skin. Jamie's skin was pristine, like the underside of a cowrie shell.

One time Cecil waved me over out front.

"You know, I just gotta tell you something," he said.

I leaned in a little closer.

"I saw your little girl out here the other day with her earplugs in and she was just singing away, 'Come on baby, ooh baby,'" he said.

Man, Cecil lit up when he told me that, his voice all sing-songy like a little girl.

I guess I could have straightened him out right there and then. But what was the point? I never corrected him. And Cecil wasn't the only one. I never really bothered correcting anybody.

I tried to smile when Cecil said he thought Jase was mine.

"Me too," I said.

Cecil took one hand from his cane and grasped my hand atop his shoulder. He just pressed it there for a moment. His grip felt strong as an oak.

"Then it's a sad day for both of us," he said.

Cecil wasn't looking at me or through me when he said that. He was looking right into me.

That Sunday I put on my best black slacks, dress shoes and a crisp white button down shirt and walked over to Christ Church. I thought about wearing a sport jacket but it was too damn hot. I always envied that one guy who gets away without wearing a suit or sport jacket. Why am I always the guy sweating in a jacket? I knew I wasn't going to know anybody anyway at Thea's memorial service, except for Cecil. What's he going to say? Where's your jacket? Maybe I'd see his daughter, the one whose name I can't remember from that day out front, but she probably won't even recognize me, or me her.

I walked the seven blocks to Christ Church. It was late September so even by five o'clock everything looked gilded by apricot sunlight. I thought a bunch about Cecil and Thea while I walked. I thought a bunch about Jamie and Jase too, like I had every day since I had met them two years ago, and every day since we moved in together last February, and every day this last week since they had moved out. It was my first Sunday without them. And I thought about why I liked the smell of alyssum so much. I nearly stepped in front of a car crossing Orange Avenue.

Christ Church was packed, every pew peopled full by folks, women with black dresses and men in suits. And I was *that* guy, the only guy without a jacket, so I stood in back at first which I think made the ushers a bit nervous. I waved off their offers to help me find a pew. I really wasn't vying for their job but after a *Reading from the Book of Isaiah* I thought it best to find a seat. By the way the ushers looked at me they agreed. Plus, they had jackets on.

The memorial pamphlet one of those old fellas handed me admonished that *The People Sit for the Readings*. After a couple sit down parts one empty pew revealed itself. Best to not break any more rules, particularly without a jacket on.

The open pew was four back, on the right, three stained-glass windows down the side aisle. Shit, it was right behind family, but some of the hymns had six verses printed out so I wasn't sure how long these Episcopalians were going to sing.

So there I ended up, not ten feet from Cecil at Thea's memorial service. Some fine Colonial Dame gave a eulogy praising Thea's long life and her love of cosmopolitans. I wished then I could have seen Thea take just one sip. I leaned forward to see how Cecil was holding up but could only see the side of his face. My view was blocked in part by a picket of balding heads that had to belong to his three sons. Cecil was being helped up and down for the sit parts by a tall gal I guessed to be his granddaughter. I couldn't place his daughter in the bunch, but she must have been there.

I liked the Reverend right away, partially because he looked like Michael Palin from Monty Python's Flying Circus and partially because he had that reverential manner of talking about death like it was part of life or something. He talked about how this was Easter for Thea, how she had gone back with the Lord and how Thea was looking down upon us now.

Jase had shown me an aerial view of our rental house on Google earth when we moved in next door to Cecil and Thea. From outer space she showed me you could actually see the red tile rooftop and the rooftop next door, plus the six twisted oaks in our narrow front lawns. Sitting in Christ Church, not ten feet from Cecil, I started thinking about those rooftops, side by side, and everything that went on beneath them.

I wondered whether a satellite could see two guys standing out front of those rooftops on the sidewalk and sharing a sad day for both of them. Did Google earth show Cecil's blue ribbon displayed in his front window? He won of course. Could it see the red ribbon taped to our front window we won for doing nothing more than signing a lease that included a gardener?

Could a satellite pick up what Cecil missed so much? Or what I missed? Sixty years to three seasons. Who was I to complain? Jamie told me last week how Jase had learned to kick the soccer ball back to her teammates when pressed by the other team. Would a satellite see that? I don't know, but maybe Comet Theodosia could see all that now. That's what the Reverend at Christ Church seemed to be talking about. And it sounded pretty good, but it didn't make me feel much better. Still, I was probably the least close person to Thea in that whole bunch of jacketed Episcopalians, so how I felt right then likely didn't matter too much.

There I was sitting in the pew, standing up, sitting back down, mumbling through some hymns, straining to see Cecil, but mostly wondering what that sixty year void must feel like. Meanwhile I was crumbling from only three seasons and wishing I could smell some alyssum. I kept on sniffling. My eyes stung. And I was sweating something fierce, even without a jacket. I don't think you could see any of that from a satellite. No way. You have to get real close for a real long time for certain stuff.

During the last hymn folks started a procession out of church one pew at a time front to back. This was the first time in a long time I actually did thank God because I needed some fresh air fast. First, Cecil left arm in arm with his granddaughter. Then his family filed out. Pretty soon I was walking down the aisle with all those black dressed and jacketed Episcopalians singing and staring at me in my sweaty white shirt and tears all over my face.

I didn't go to the reception. I needed to get out of there. So I walked back home all by myself. I took off my sweaty clothes and sat in my underwear in the living room awhile. I just sat there in silence. No Jamie, no Jase, no cats running all over me. I didn't call anybody. I didn't text anybody. I didn't turn on the TV or any music.

I walked into Jase's old bedroom. It used to be a constant mess of clothes and books and stuffed animals and crumpled homework and candy wrappers and cat hair and attitude and all that ten-year-old girl stuff. Her bed was always pushed askew and rarely made. She used to always try and hide her mess under the covers. Smart little gal.

Now Jase's bedroom is my writing room: a bare desk, chair, laptop and a purple yoga mat rolled up on the hardwoods. Serene. Empty. I'm just starting to get up the nerve to sit in there and let some words come out. I never know what those words are going to be, or where they come from. What stories do I have anyway?

I want to go over and have that martini with Cecil. I want to put my hand back on his shoulder and hear him tell me sixty years of Thea stories. I'll go over every night if I have to. But what I really want is to sip sixty years of martinis with my own Thea.

But we lost Thea on Tuesday.

We really did.

Horror Writer

Loree Hill

Rigid fingers pound
with rancor and malice
clackity clack clack
old typewriter keys
hammer hard and fast
beating letters from
an inked ribbon full of words
waiting to be released
a moment before
being trapped for eternity
on a paper's pocked face.

Little Harry Morose

Jesse Robinson

All three Morose children were home schooled in a Christian madrasah facilitated by their mother, Headmistress Clair Lily Morose, wife of evangelical dentist Dr. Horrid Lee Morose Sr., a successful biblically based, drug free pediatric dentist.

Sullen Morose, the oldest boy at fourteen never was quite the same after his punitive root canal for uttering the word *dinosaur* at age six. And till this very day he still talks as if he has cotton in his mouth.

Regretta Morose, the middle child, was born with a severe clubfoot, ovoid in shape. Her parents refused postnatal surgery telling pediatric ortho that the Almighty wants their daughter to teach karate with her weaponized lower limb.

The youngest, Horrid Lee Morose Jr., little Harry for short, the precocious young boy lost his eye by secretly experimenting with vinegar and baking soda inside a Sonkissed Heavenly Soda bottle.

The cap shot the curious little boy so deeply in the eye socket that it corked the wound shut, rendering it almost bloodless.

Hearing the commotion, Regretta pivoted on the apex of her prehistoric egg shaped God gift, and furiously rock-walked out back taking a knee next to her mother who was already on the scene reminding the writhing little boy for the umpteenth time that Jesus hates science.

Regretta removed her Shroud of Turin commemorative handkerchief from the front pocket of her caraco jacket and gently cleaned the residual blood around her brother's eye before she and her mother pried it open to assess the loving God's marksmanship. Harry, squirmed silently in place, dug in his heels and fainted as Regretta rolled up her Holy Hanky dabbing and blotting the back of his eye socket like she was drying the bottom of a tall glass. Her jaw dropped as she took the first look into her little brother's head.

"I think that Jesus shot Harry in the eye with the winning Sweepstakes Cap," said Regretta, compelling Headmistress Morose to gasp in disbelief.

"Don't fuck with me Regretta," she exclaimed on the exhale, pulling her daughter aside by the back of her Mennonite made neck doily.

Clair Lily Morose looked inside her little boy's head for herself and compared the sacred seven numbers on the cap in her child's head to those on the back label of the soda bottle lying next to her child's head.

"Jesus shot him dead square in the eye with the winning sweepstakes' cap!" concurred Clair Lily jumping for joy as Regretta hopped awkwardly on her God giftless good leg for joy over the little heathen's body.

The doctors had to wait for the pressure to subside before they could remove the cap from Harry's head. One small problem, that cap had to be in Chicago Headquarters in three days or it expired. So Harry's family discharged the boy and flew him to Chicago where each elder from corporate lifted up the patch and gauze and looked into Harry's head with little flashlights to physically authenticate that Jesus did indeed shoot little Harry in the eye with the winning Sonkissed Heavenly Soda Sweepstakes Cap.

Once and Now

Nazli Ghassemi

Once the fervor of youth,
Once the unending dreams of unattainable love,
Once the warrior surpassing barriers,
Once fiery zest of life,
Once the herculean deeds,

Now an ageing body,
Now the table,
Now the slippery floor,
Now the long walk to the bathroom,
Now the trapped air inside,
Now the loud helpless roar,
Of the once wild beast within.

About the Editors

reg e. gaines (Poetry): This Tony-nominated writer, for the Broadway hit *Bring in Da Noise/Bring in Da Funk,* reg e gaines has facilitated his popular, "Is Poetry Theater?" workshops during various residencies including, The University of Southern California, Oregon Shakespeare Festival, The New Jersey Performing Arts Center, Los Angeles Windward School, The Nuyorican Poets Café, Voz Alta Project Gallery, The World Stage, Beyond Baroque, Farleigh Dickinson University, Rosa Parks Performing Arts Academy, Passaic County Community College, Montclair Public Library, and Scratch DJ Academy, which he co-founded with Jam Master Jay and Rob Principe.

Dean Nelson (Prose): Dr. Dean Nelson is the founder and director of the journalism program at PLNU. He writes occasionally for the New York Times, the Boston Globe, Christianity Today, Sojourners, and several other national publications. He has won several awards from the Society of Professional Journalists for his reporting, and has written or co-written 11 books. He has traveled throughout the world covering stories of human interest, including India, where he wrote about the slums of Bombay; Kosovo, where he interviewed and wrote about victims of terrorism; Africa, where he wrote about members of the Black Panther Party who live in exile in Tanzania; Tibet, where he wrote about religious persecution; and Central America, where he wrote about poverty and contaminated water. In addition to directing the PLNU journalism program, Nelson also hosts the annual Writer's Symposium By The Sea, where prominent writers come to discuss the craft of writing.

Contributors

Anita Knowles, originally from Ohio, considers both the Midwest and San Diego home. She works in veterinary medicine and is writing a novel about life on the Ohio home front, World War II. Passionately devoted to her pup, Rizzo, she is a rabid fan of Duke Basketball, *Supernatural*, and dry wit.

Anitra Carol Smith, born at an early age/has played terrifying flute solos/finds solace in composing disreputable boogie woogie tunes/journalist, biographer, humanities teacher/lefthanded vegan text synesthete/fabric artist/Kelee meditator/Occidental College,UCSD/published currently in *Stone Voices* literary journal/has a novel titled *Kippy and Claude* in the hopper.

Anne Canter writes poetry and nonfiction, plays roller derby and works for Just Like My Child Foundation. Born in Colorado, she graduated from Northwestern University in 2011, and has lived in San Diego ever since. Influences include Joan Didion, Kay Ryan, and Dorothy Parker. She writes at annecanter.com.

Barbara Huntington, with four grown children and seven grandchildren, Barbara was a civil rights worker, teacher, early computing company CEO, technical writer, marketing analyst/consultant, and recently retired as Director of Preprofessional Health Advising at SDSU. She has a BS in Zoology from SDSU and an MBA from UCLA. She lives in Chula Vista with her puppy, Tashi, an organic vegetable garden, and a labyrinth of rocks and succulents.

Carrie Danielson taught English in Chula Vista, California. Now retired, she has time to explore her life-long desire to write. Born and raised in Colorado, her first career was acting and directing in local Colorado theaters. She is grateful to SDWI for their support of writers and this opportunity.

Chloe Sparacino was born in Los Angeles, and she received her B.A. in English from Madonna University. She lives in San Diego and writes creative nonfiction and poetry. In addition to her blog, *Real Awkward Words*, her work has also appeared in *Manor House Quarterly* and *Viewpoint Magazine*.

Christina Dorudian has been writing poetry since she was a child. She also loves writing short stories and is currently revising her first novel. She has been published in *Writers' Journal, Highlights, Sparkle*, and local newspapers. When she's not writing, reading, or teaching school, she enjoys spending time with her husband, two sons, and dog.

Claudia Poquoc began her formal study of poetry at Writers Haven in San Diego in 1987. She hosts the Bluestocking women's poetry revision group and teaches poetry to elementary school children in Southern California. Her first song and poetry book, *Becomes Her Vision*, includes a CD. Her latest book, *Keeper of the Fields*, was published in September of 2014. Her poems appear in the San Diego Poetry Annual, San Diego Writers, Ink, and Magee Park anthologies, and other publications.

Clayton Truscott is a South African travel, surf, and fiction writer. He has an MA in Creative Writing from the University of Cape Town and currently works as a freelance writer in San Diego. His books are available at www.claytontruscott.com.

Dania Brett is a mid-city based artist and writer. She has worked in education and social services, and feels that her experiences in each inform…and fuel her art. Dania views the creative process as a meditation, exploring the relationships we have with ourselves, one another, and the world.

David Raines is a writer, actor, and graphic designer. He hales from Placerville, California where his introduction to Stephen King sparked his interest in writing. He currently lives in San

Diego where he pursues his acting and writing passions.

Debbie Hall is a writer whose poetry has appeared in *City Works Literary Journal, A Year in Ink, Vol. 5, Servinghouse Journal,* and *Swamp Lily Review.* Her essays have appeared on NPR (*This I Believe* series), in *USD Magazine,* and the *San Diego Union Tribune.*

Diane Malloy, M.S.W., is a published writer, teacher, group facilitator, and fun-lover who runs the popular Pen to Paper class at the La Jolla Library. She also develops and teaches classes on various topics for non-profits and business groups. She volunteers, dances, acts, and loves life.

Elizabeth Forsyth is a native San Diegan. She is currently writing her first novel, *Ed(uardo),* and pursuing a certificate in creative writing from UCLA. When Elizabeth is not writing, she enjoys playing music, drinking tea, and chasing squirrels away from her garden.

Frank Primiano worked as an engineer, professor, and entrepreneur and has been published in professional journals and textbooks. He lived in Philadelphia and Cleveland before moving to San Diego with his wife, Elaine. Frank was a finalist in the SD Book Awards 2008 Unpublished Novel and 2013 Unpublished Short Story competitions.

Fred Longworth never recovered from the dire influences of *Mad Magazine.* He holds an A.B. in English Literature (SDSU), and an MBA (National University). Obligatory poetry credits: *Able Muse, Bloodroot, California Quarterly, Comstock Review, Pearl, Rattapallax, Spillway, Stirring,* and "et al." Frankly, his life has mostly consisted of "etc" and "et al." Go figure.

James M. McCollum is a member of San Diego Writers, Ink and also a retired airline pilot. He flew medical evacuation helicopters in Vietnam in 1968 and 1969. His poetry has been published in *A Year in Ink, Volume 6, The San Diego Poetry Annual,* and literary magazines. He has been invited to read his poetry at schools, book stores, book clubs, and the Solana Beach Public Library. When not writing, he is a volunteer tutor at La Clase Magica, an after school homework tutoring program in Solana Beach.

Jesse Robinson is a local writer, father of two, and published author of two best selling self help books, *I Am Your Life Coach.... Quit!* and *5 Simple Steps to Losing Your Will and Ending It All.* This fall is the release of his autobiography, *The Great Recession: My Battle and Defeat In The War on Male Pattern Baldness.*

Jill G. Hall is a visual artist as well as a writer. Her poems have been inspired by the nature's awe, romances gone bad and good, and life's ironies. *The Black Velvet Coat*, her first novel, is due to be published in Fall 2015 by She Writes Press. Her essays on the art of practicing a creative lifestyle can be found at www.jillghall.com.

Jim Moreno is on the Program Committee and teaches poetry workshops for SDWI, the Juvenile Court and Community Schools, and Young Audiences of San Diego. He is the director of Cultural Circle Poetry Workshops and hosts an open mic at the Cafe Cabaret, 2nd Tuesday-Jihmye Poetry.

John Castell, a fine artist and writer of creative nonfiction and memoir, he received his BFA from Parsons School of Design, NYC and was recipient of the Ellen Battel Stoeckel Trust Fellowship Award to YALE at Norfolk. He lives in San Diego with his husband.

Judy Reeves is a writer, teacher, and writing practice provacateur who has published four books on the subject including *A Writer's Book of Days.* Her newest book, *Wild Women, Wild Voices*, will be released in April, 2015. She has always wanted to be a singer.

Kenneth Zak was born in Parma, Ohio. His debut novel, *The Poet's Secret*, will be published in 2015 by Penju Publishing. The poem *Two Bits* from *The Poet's Secret* previously appeared in *Kelp Magazine* and his short fiction *A Promise* appeared in *A Year in Ink, Vol. 4.*

Lawrence Richard Carleton has published or otherwise presented scholarly work in philosophy, cognitive science, and software development. He has recently turned to fiction, with a preference for tales highlighting social issues. Several of his flash fictions appear in *The Guilded Pen*, the San Diego Writers/ Editors Guild's annual anthology.

Linda Hutchison is a freelance writer living in La Jolla, California. She has worked as a newspaper journalist, an advertising copywriter, and a technical writer. She is the author of two books for high school students, *Lebanon* and *Finland*. Her poems have appeared in several journals. She blogs at www.headwindjournal.com.

Loree Hill is a writer of fiction, character development, poetry, personal essay. Her words have been published in the *Magee Park Poets Anthology 2013, empowher.com, In Our Words Writers, Survivor's Review,* and *A Year in Ink, Vol. 8.*

Lynn Gahman funded her piano studies with forays into construction, consumer finance, and bartending before becoming an entertainer. Turning from song styling to the written word, Gahman appears in literary journals, local newspapers, and digital media. Her quirky humor is fueled by living abroad, her entertainment experiences, and her eclectic lifestyle.

Mark Tuller lives in Encinitas. Before he retired, he was a lawyer for Verizon Wireless in New Jersey. He moved to California with his wife to try something totally different, and he took up poetry.

Martha Kinkade is a visionary writer. For her, writing is a spiritual practice. Her first book of poems, *Winter's Light* (*Montezuma Publishing 2011*), documents the contradictions found in her Wyoming youth. Her poetry has appeared in *Psychic Meatloaf, Jackson Hole Review, A Year in Ink,* and *The Mom Egg.*

Mary Fry is a novelist, screenwriter, and poet. Her book of poems, *Adobe Doorways,* was conferred the Pegasus Award for creative writing. Other poems have appeared in the literary journal *The Brushfire*. Her screenplay, *Denim & da Vinci*, has caught the attention of Hollywood. You can visit her at www. MaryJFry.com.

Michael W. Berns, Ph.D. is Professor of Bioengineering at UC San Diego and Irvine. He received his undergraduate and graduate degrees from Cornell University. He has written over four hundred research articles about using lasers to study cells and disease. His work has been featured in *National Geographic* and *Scientific American* magazines.

Michael Evangelista is a high school senior attending Mira Mesa High. He is the co-president of MMHS' Creative Writing Club and a semifinalist for Scholastic's National Student Poets Program. In his free time, he enjoys writing poems, making short films, and spending time with his lovely pet fish, Samantha.

Mike Hedrick had a tenth grade English teacher who taught modern poetry with her hair on fire. He's been writing ever since. SoCal boy all his life; UCLA grad with a BA in English; published in *The Christian Science Monitor, City Lights,* and *California Quarterly.*

Nancy Dimsdale is a fledgling poet whose work has appeared in the *Magee Park Poets Anthology.*

Nazli Ghassemi wrote her first novel, *Desert Mojito*, while working and living in Dubai. She has traveled extensively and has worked variously as a dance instructor, businesswoman, translator, and ESL teacher. She also has a degree in Biomedical Engineering from UC, San Diego. She works and lives in San Diego.

Penelope James is an Anglo-Mexican-American and a former advertising executive in New York, London, and Mexico City. She has worked as a Hispanic research report writer, translator, columnist, book editor, and co-author of two books. Author of *Don't Hang Up! On the Border of A New Start* to be published spring 2015. She currently resides in San Diego, CA.

Rebecca Romani is currently at large in Southern California where she teaches film and covers art, culture, and politics for a variety of publications.

Regina Morin is a long time resident of Ocean Beach. An original member of the Border Voices Poetry Project, her poems have appeared in *Visions Magazine, America, San Diego Writer's Monthly, Magee Park Poets Anthology, A Year in Ink,* and *The Reader*. Born into Clan O'Connell, she is deeply disturbed by the misuse, abuse, and absence of apostrophes that she encounters daily in posted signs and text.

Ron Salisbury is a writer living in San Diego and a student in SDSU's MFA program, Creative Writing. Publications and awards include: *Eclipse, The Cape Reader, Serving House Journal, The San Diego Reader, Alaska Quarterly Review, Spitball, Soundings East,* etc; semi-finalist for the Anthony Hecht Poetry Prize 2012, finalist for the ABZ First Book Contest 2014.

Seretta Martin is an artist, poet, and editor, teaches workshops at SDWI, libraries, museums, and schools. She is a short-list finalist for *Philip Levine* and *Washington* prizes. Author: *Foreign Dust Familiar Rain* and forthcoming books. Published: *Web del Sol, Serving House, Margie, Modern Haiku, California Quarterly, City Works, Pl, SDPA,* and others.

Shannon Bates is a musician and writer originally from Fair Oaks, California. She writes fiction and is currently working toward her MFA in Creative Writing at the Rainier Writing Workshop at Pacific Lutheran University. And you may rest assured that she's wearing something green right now. Perhaps many green things.

Steve Bruno has always been a serious romantic. He began writing love stories about ten years ago. In 2014 two of his novels, *Martha* and *Earth Angel* were published by *Lot's Cave* under the nom de plume of Jeff DeLuna. *Kissing Rosalie* spawned *Earth Angel*.

Sumilu Cue's disillusionment with a legal career prompted her to become a professional artist. She is a writer, printmaker, and (very) amateur musician. This is her first publication in the SDWI anthology.

Sylvia Levinson's poetry life began while working at the Old Globe Theatre. She is the author of *Spoon* (*Finishing Line Press*) and *Gateways* (*Caernarvon Press*). Publications include: *Blue Arc West, City Works, A Year in Ink, Magee Park, Christian Science Monitor, The Reader, Serving House Journal*. She believes 'retirement' is an active verb.

Sylvia J. Nelson is 58 years old with four sons and 23+ grandchildren. She's lived in California 29 years. Nana Nelson attends Southwestern College for a degree in Business Administration and Teaching. She sings in church choir and helps with the children's choir. However, she's passionate about writing.

Tania Pryputniewicz recently appeared in *Poetry Flash* and *Soundings East*. Her debut collection, *November Butterfly*, was published by *Saddle Road Press* (2014). Tania teaches poetry and blogging for San Diego Writers, Ink. She lives in Coronado with her husband, three children, one Siberian Husky, and two tubby housecats.

Tim Calaway lives in San Diego writing poetry, short stories, and novels. He is currently working on his next novel. He can be heard reading his work at Dimestories and Poetic Brew.

Tina Culp Barton, an empty nester, in 2009 realized that she had better do something with her time before she drove her husband crazy. So she started writing poetry. Her work has appeared in numerous publications. Tina lives in Pacific Beach with her husband, Tom, and their desert tortoise, Maggie. tcbpoetry@aol.com.

About San Diego Writers, Ink

San Diego Writers, Ink, serves as a hub for the literary communty, promotes literature, provides artistic development for writers at all levels, and facilitates artistic collaboration. A 501(c)(3) nonprofit organization, SDWI offers classes, groups, workshops, readings, and other literary events at The Ink Spot and other locations throughout San Diego County.

San Diego Writers, Ink   The Ink Spot
www.SanDiegoWriters.org   2730 Historic Decatur Rd. #202
                              San Diego, CA 92106
                              (619) 696-0363

A Year in Ink, an anthology published each year by San Diego Writers, Ink, represents a sampling of our community's most brilliant work. Each volume includes shorts stories, novel and memoir excerpts, creative nonfiction, satire, flash fiction, poetry, and more. The authors are a diverse group of young and old, new writers and much-published veterans. Several have had work in previous anthologies, most have been published in other literary journals, and a few allow A Year in Ink the honor of showcasing their first publication.

Explore the complete A Year in Ink collection available at our website.

A Year in Ink, Volume 1 (2008), edited by Thomas Larson

A Year in Ink, Volume 2 (2009), edited by Sandra Alcosser
    and Arthur Salm

A Year in Ink, Volume 3 (2010), edited by Roger Aplon and
Jennifer Silva Redmond

A Year in Ink, Volume 4 (2011), edited by Jericho Brown and
Laurel Corona

A Year in Ink, Volume 5 (2012), edited by Brandon Cesmat
and T. Greenwood

A Year in Ink, Volume 6 (2013), edited by Michael Klam and
Anthony Bonds

A Year in Ink, Volume 7 (2014), edited by Shadab Zeest
Hashmi and Jim Ruland

A Year in Ink, Volume 8 (2015), edited by reg e gains and
Dean Nelson

www.ingramcontent.com/pod-product-compliance
Lightning Source LLC
Chambersburg PA
CBHW070935250626
47159CB00009B/3256